THE WITCH'S GUIDE
TO MANIFESTATION

THE
WITCH'S
GUIDE TO
MANIFESTATION

WITCHCRAFT
FOR THE LIFE
YOU WANT

Mystic Dylan

ILLUSTRATIONS BY TARA O'BRIEN

**ROCKRIDGE
PRESS**

Interior and Cover Designer: Patricia Fabricant
Art Producer: Samantha Ulban
Editor: Sean Newcott
Illustrations © 2021 Tara O'Brien. Author Photo Courtesy of Olivia Graves

Paperback ISBN: 978-1-64876-350-2 | eBook ISBN: 978-1-64876-351-9
R0

To those new to the path of witchcraft, and to those who came before us. To my parents, my grandmother, and my fierce friends and mentors, who have supported and encouraged me.

CONTENTS

INTRODUCTION

If you've stumbled across this book, it's probably for a reason. Actually, I'd even dare to say you've manifested it somehow. How, you ask? We will get into that a bit later. In your hands, you currently hold a tome of magic, a key to unlocking your powers and obtaining everything you desire. Think of this book as a guide to unleashing your power.

Whether you are aware of it or not, you manifest things all the time. Ever wish on a star? Or thrown a coin into a fountain while making a wish? Even if you don't think you've ever cast a spell or practiced magic, the truth is that those scenarios are examples of folk magic. Making a wish and blowing out the candle on a birthday cake is another common custom. And it, too, is a form of magic. Aside from the magical act itself, even the origins of the tradition are magical. It began with the ancient Greeks, who made small, round cakes dedicated to Artemis, the goddess of the moon. The cakes were lit by candles, and prayers and petitions would be made as the candles were blown out so that the smoke could carry the wishes up to the goddess. So, I bet you've cast a spell or two in your lifetime.

My first introduction to magic began quite early in my childhood. I remember sitting in my grandmother's backyard, overlooking the dock in Florida, feeling the buzz and vibrations of another realm. If I squinted my eyes enough, I swear I could see fairies fluttering about the tall sea grape tree. I was constantly playing alone, yet chatting it up with friends who were invisible to everyone but me. My grandparents encouraged my love of mythology, as did my parents, who would read me tales of hidden realms, fierce gods and goddesses, and witches who could draw the moon down with the muttering of a chant.

On one auspicious day, my mother took me to a shop in Los Angeles called Panpipes (a.k.a. Pan's Apothika), where I met a real witch for the first time. The owner, Vicky, forever changed the course of my life. Watching her craft a candle and looking around the shop, I knew that nothing would ever be the same. From that day on, I read any book on witchcraft I could get my hands on. After years of studying and solitary practice, I eventually became initiated into a coven, and several covens after that.

Today, I practice what is called traditional witchcraft, which is based heavily on historical recordings of witch trials, folklore, and folk magic. I also incorporate elements from my heritage into my craft to honor my Cuban, Irish, German, French, and Native American ancestors. The spirits and deities I work with synchronize with each other and revealed themselves to me in dreams and omens.

In this book, you'll learn what manifestation is, how to accomplish it, and how to use it alongside witchcraft, spellwork, and rituals. You will find correspondences and charts to aid in your workings, as well as help you craft and create your own spells. Let's dive in and make some magic.

CHAPTER 1

On Magic & Manifestation

"Magic, indeed, is all around us, in stones, flowers, stars, the dawn wind, and the sunset cloud; all we need is the ability to see and understand."

—DOREEN VALIENTE

Magic. The word itself stimulates the senses and vibrates with energy. It is a word that has been defined in many different ways by many different people over the centuries. However, it is not just a word, but also a spell, a gift, and a primordial spirit that has been around since the dawn of time. It is within these pages that you will learn how to establish a relationship with manifestation and magic, two arcane concepts you'll soon learn to use for your own benefit.

What is magic? What is manifestation? And how are these concepts integral to your practice and to manifesting your desires? To answer those questions, we must first go back millennia, to when humans, gods, and nature first made their pact with each other. In this chapter, you'll learn not only the definition of magic, but also its history and connection to manifestation.

What Is Magic?

Put simply, magic is a force in the universe that is used to manipulate energy and nature. Magic itself comes from nature, and just like nature, it is neither good nor evil. Magic—and the urge to manipulate it—has existed from the earliest creation. When properly harnessed, magic can assist you in achieving your desired goal. It can be used to remove obstacles, help you get that promotion, strengthen the relationship you have with your partner, and attract new friends and financial opportunities. Magic cannot make you levitate, resurrect the dead, or force someone to love you. Magic is meant to be used alongside physical and mundane work, not in place of it. For example, if you wish to use magic to get a job, you must also make an attempt to get the job by applying. Magic will not get you the job out of the blue.

By now, you might be asking, "Well, what is witch-craft?" Witchcraft is the practice and use of magic. That's it. Despite what many people often assume, witchcraft is not a religion; it is a practice that may or may not be part of a person's spiritual or religious faith.

Today, the term "witchcraft" is often used interchange-ably with "Wicca," a Neo-Pagan religion that started in England during the 20th century and was introduced to the public in 1954 by Gerald Gardner. Not all witches are

Wiccan. The witchcraft that I practice and refer to in these pages is not to be conflated with Wicca, and is more akin to traditional witchcraft and folk magic.

Witchcraft is the use of magic to achieve a desired outcome. Magic is a neutral force and witchcraft is a neutral practice. That means that witchcraft, like magic, is neither "good" nor "evil." Like any other tool, witchcraft can be used with malice, or it can be used to heal. Witchcraft is entirely conditional upon the motives of the practitioner. For this reason, it is crucial to be sure of your intentions when casting a spell. It is also important to note that like the concept of "good and evil," the terms "black magic" and "white magic" should also be removed from your vocabulary when referring to the craft. These terms carry racial connotations and stigma, and are not integral to the real practice of witchcraft.

Anyone can be a witch and practice witchcraft and magic. While there is no bloodline you have to be a part of, we all have Pagan ancestors who practiced some sort of folk magic if you go back far enough. Witchcraft is open to everyone regardless of race, religion, ethnicity, ability, sexual orientation, or gender identity. However, witchcraft has no room for racism, patriarchy, homophobia, transphobia, xenophobia, ableism, etc., as those views and mentalities defy the natural order of unity and equality to which witchcraft and magic adhere.

Witches and magic practitioners draw their energies from nature. Some of us may work with deities, while others might not. Witchcraft is a secular practice, and therefore doesn't adhere to any religious or dogmatic principles. Magic and witchcraft has been practiced all over the world for millennia. Not all witches adhere to one specific school of thought. Culture, region, history, and preference shape different aspects of the craft. For example, if you have a strong connection to plants, then herb craft and nature magic might resonate with you.

History & Use of Magical Manifestation

◇◇◇◇◇◇◇◇◇◇◇◇◇

Magic was conceived when man lit the first spark that created a flame. Magic was there when willow bark was first used in 1500 BCE as a pain reliever by the ancient Egyptians. Magic is present when a child is delivered safely into the world.

Magic itself is almost synonymous with manifestation. The strength of human desire and the seemingly "miraculous" ability to achieve those desires gave birth to the idea of magic and manifestation. Today, we might be more familiar with the term "law of attraction"; however, this ideology wasn't fully fleshed out till the 19th century. Manifestation is part of many ancient practices and Eastern philosophies. While it wasn't called "manifestation" in antiquity, it was frequently referenced in Buddhist manuscripts and early Christian texts.

The modern belief and practice of magic in Western culture predominantly stems from Kemetic (ancient Egyptian) Greco-Roman, Celtic, and Judeo-Christian beliefs and religion.

The root word for *"magic"* (Greek: *mageia*; Latin: *magia*) comes from the ancient Greek word *magoi*, which referred to a Median tribe in Persia and their religion, Zoroastrianism. During the Greco-Roman era, it was believed that magicians possessed arcane knowledge and could channel power from or through any of the deities, spirits, or ancestors of the ancient pantheons, a belief and practice that survives today in Neo-Pagan, Wiccan, and traditional witchcraft practices. Many traditions associated with magic in the modern world derive from a fascination with ancient customs and beliefs, and are intermingled with a need for counter-magic against sorcery, spirits, fairies, or witches. The need for spells to be written down, uttered, or spoken aloud gave birth to the manifestation concept that "words have power."

Late in the 19th century, due to several Victorian authors, scholars, and philosophers, manifestation came to be seen as a pseudoscience. Helena Blavatsky, a Russian philosopher and author who was involved in the spiritualist movement and deeply interested in the occult, was key to bringing the idea of manifestation to the mainstream.

Blavatsky traveled across the world studying different metaphysical teachings, and gained a reputation for being extraordinarily spiritually gifted. She drew on ancient religious ceremonies, rituals, and traditions to write a book called *The Secret Doctrine*. Much of what she believed coincided with what we now call "the law of attraction." She argued that our opinions about ourselves and our identity define who we are and what we're capable of. Thomas Troward, another 19th-century author whose work is widely believed to have influenced many contemporary law of attraction monographs, including *The Secret*, has been described by many modern-day scholars as a "mystic Christian." Many 20th-century authors and spiritualists published their unique takes on the concept of manifestation in the decades that followed. The majority of these authors illustrate their beliefs with examples of success in their own lives.

Today, manifestation and magic are concepts that most are well acquainted with. While the concept of manifestation at its core is about manipulating energy to achieve specific outcomes, pairing it with magic lends us additional power to fuel our intent. Manifestation is a tool for shaping both our outer and inner realities. Truly, manifestation is now rediscovering its magic.

How Does It Work?

Witchcraft is the intentional use of magic while upholding tradition and folklore. Tradition and folklore are so incredibly different for every individual because they can be based on location, lived experience, and ancestry. The practice of magic in general involves offering yourself a natural focal point to engage with your surroundings and an intentional vision of your life.

You and I are points in time; we are events. Magic is a feature of the event of your life. It can alter how the event takes place. The way in which you decide to use magic is up to you. Because you are offering a focal point for your event in magic, you are offering your life event a theme. This theme that we offer ourselves gives us an idea of what to look for in our waking world and helps us present an energy that draws to us what we most desire.

You may have heard of the idea of being on a vibrational wavelength that resonates positively with other aspects of the universe. Energy is attached to our emotions. I'm sure you've met someone with an energy that you're drawn to or repelled by. Manifestation magic is about accessing the energy—the vibration/wavelength—that also holds our desires.

Part of this stems from the idea of sympathetic magic—the subconscious search for corresponding stimuli, and those stimuli that we only find when we are actively looking for them. Part of having a magical focus is opening a gateway to the sympathetic magic of relation, teaching ourselves a new way to view the world. The way you view the world is intrinsically linked to the energy you offer the stimuli you take in. Are you offering that bad driver a good flip of the bird, or are you letting it go in favor of seeing your lucky number on their license plate? Maybe you walk in the middle and see the neutral road—your middle finger is a 1, they have a 1 on their license plate, and your lucky number is 11. Regardless, positive thought allows us to access positive magic, and positive magic manifests good in our lives, whereas negative thought can manifest harm in our lives or the lives of those to whom we offer that energy.

Non-Magical Methods of Manifesting

The mundane is unavoidable and necessary, and because of that, manifestation is more than just a mystic practice; it has roots in reality, in the way we live. Gardening is an example of very literal productive manifestation. The gardener is an alchemist, combining knowledge and a ritual practice of timing, seeding, and caretaking to manifest fruitful plants. Whatever it is that we'd like to manifest requires intent and care, like plants in a garden. Things like vision boarding, journaling, envisioning, embodying, using a focus wheel, or literally spelling out your intention are all ways to let the universe know what you'd like to manifest and bring you closer to your desires. When there's no physical garden to tend, find other ways to nourish your manifesting intentions.

VISION BOARDING

This is a powerful way to create the aesthetic of your desire. Your vision board will also be incredibly individualized and distinctly different from someone else's vision board, even if you're both trying to manifest the same thing. There are so many ways to assemble a collection of images centered around your goal, including a collage. Vision board collages provide inspiring imagery that we offer meaning to, and they serve as reminders of what we want, to help us address where we are and where we're going. They're fantastic to keep in a personally high-traffic area, such as on top of a dresser, by the door, and even in the bathroom if you're pressed for space. Vision boards help us continue to think about our goal, and they allow us to see it daily, which makes us more likely to take actions that move our goals forward.

Take some time to create a vision board! Print out pictures, take some scissors to a few old magazines, and break out the glue and tape. Do not inhibit yourself with thinking too hard about other people's vision boards. This is about what your goal looks like to you. Once you have collected images, words, shapes, and phrases that you think suit your goal, lay them out on posterboard before committing to their placement. Once you are happy with the way everything looks, start taping, gluing, or pinning it all in place.

INTENTION/GRATITUDE
JOURNALING

Our thoughts need to go somewhere. Most of us do not say everything that comes to mind. Sometimes, our thoughts and feelings are just for us. The practice of journaling can help us feel listened to by the person that we need most—our inner selves. The very intentional act of journaling desires and gratitude communicates to our inner selves what aspects of our lives should change. Consider what you are grateful for to invite more good into your life, and how your manifestation desires will improve your life. Keeping these thoughts in a journal provides a tangible point of reference for your own internal world, and in a way, it becomes a written map, laying out the journey to your dreams.

Think about what you are most grateful for, from events and people to sights, smells, sounds, and feelings. Write down at least five things you are truly grateful for. Consider what you desire most deeply and write it down in simple words. Now, let's write a story. It can be symbolic or as realistic as you like, but pretend you are telling this story to your child-self. Your goal in this story is your goal in your real world, though, if it helps to offer a metaphor, you could give it a fantasy setting. Think about what details most excite your inner child. What is your inner child most afraid of, and how can you overcome that while including what you are grateful for in your story line? Your story can be one page in length or many pages.

VISUALIZATION

All of your senses can aid in your visualization process. It is about creating a time and place that you want to be inside of your mind. It is a spot of refuge and anticipation where you can develop the world as you would like to see it. This will help you gain a clearer idea of what you want and what you need to do as time goes on to achieve that. This should be a relaxing and productive station, a meditative process. If you want an Emmy, visualize having an Emmy, not the pomp of the awards ceremony. This type of looking ahead is about preparing for our desired future.

Create your space, give yourself room to breathe, close your eyes, relax, and imagine the layout of the place you most want to be. Start off with an empty room. If your ideal space is outdoors, imagine that you remove the walls from around you and free yourself into nature. Place a window and a door where you wish. Have as many windows as you want—a skylight, even. Start to fill your space, maybe with things that are familiar to you. If you'd like to have technology in this space, consider the gentle hum of electricity, perhaps the sound of houseplants shifting gently in the breeze from your open window. What does it look like outside? What does the table you have your items on feel like? Is there carpeting, tile, sand, or grass? This is a space where anything is possible. Let yourself stay in this space for as long as you like, imagining every detail down to the scent of the candle you would most like to have there. When you feel ready to come back out, imagine yourself walking out the door, or down a path that leads you out. Write down a bit about that space, or even speak about it out loud to yourself to better access it next time.

OTHER METHODS

Of course, these are not the only methods of manifestation we have; they are just the most common, and as individuals, different methods are going to work differently for each of us. Some people like a method called Bedtime Reprogramming, which allows you to play out your desires in your sleep. Some people also use affirmations, and those can be short-term and long-term goal-setting affirmations. Third-person visualization lets us get an idea of how we want to appear in our day-to-day. There is also writing letters from your future self, as a sort of projection to reach forward and retrieve guidance from the place you would like to be. You can also try abstracting your own methods from the ones you are most drawn to.

LAW OF ATTRACTION

The law of attraction is a metaphysical philosophy that assigns energies to thoughts. Our thoughts so often create direction for our feelings. We want to access positive thoughts to feel positive things and draw in positive energy. While the law of attraction may seem simple on the surface, there is a lot of personal work that is necessitated by this. Some of us who enjoy the magical aspects of life may call this "shadow work," which refers to the often difficult and intimate work that you need to do for yourself to move forward. Not only does the law of attraction ask us to make corrections and adjustments to our internal voice, but to our external voice as well. To change something also is to know it, so get to know your critical self to dissect what you are experiencing.

The idea of the suspension of disbelief is necessary, as disbelief is limiting. We have all been told magic isn't real, but to open ourselves up to the possibility of reaching our dreams and incorporating spellwork into our manifesting efforts, we must eliminate limiting thought patterns.

Once we do that, we can create true magic. The law of attraction is, in a way, the mundane and invisible ingredient to all spellwork. So, part of your homework and part of your practice should be offering up more faith in yourself and in your own magic. You are a magical being, and it is time to question what exactly is holding you back from feeling worthy of your goals. Removing these blockages will help you act more swiftly and confidently in the face of the opportunity that your spellwork could magically draw in. Plus, nothing draws in connection to like-minded people like also being aware of who you are and how you move through the world.

This book is a guide on the way to manifestation. Magic is part of your story, and if you want to include magic in your manifestation and healing process, this book offers a wonderful way to go about doing that. The things that the law of attraction asks us to do for ourselves are necessary ingredients to contentment, regardless of their magical or mundane qualities.

The law of attraction says that positive and negative are different sums to different people; what is positive to you may be negative to someone else and vice versa. Dreams are often big. Think about the details of your dreams and how what you put out affects the world all around you. Dream big, but adapt with kind consideration for the livelihoods of other people. Some people dream of being politicians or business owners, and those are people who can create massive positive and negative change for others. The same applies to owners of large and lucrative businesses. Your dreams present an opportunity not just to live how you wish, but also to be a positive force in the world.

Psychology

A good friend of mine likes to say, "If you meet two assholes in a day, just look in the mirror to see the third." It's a profane but profound piece of wisdom. The law of attraction asks us to shift perspective. Maybe that barista at the coffee shop seemed to be giving you attitude when they're actually just exhausted from a long day. We've all had good intentions but little to no energy to give someone an overtly positive interaction. Maybe the person that cut you off did it by accident in one of those petrifying moments of silly social panic we all experience on the road. It's all about how we decide to view things in the moment.

Letting a barista or fellow driver elicit a negative reaction from us sets us up to experience more negativity, because that is the vibration being emitted. As a direct result, that person may become more negative, which creates an endless cycle of more negativity and negative responses.

The positive or neutral thought-projecting person is not constantly ruminating on the bad; they are not stuck between the rock and the hard place that they create. This allows them to be more open to opportunity, because they are not spending energy fuming about the past or expecting a terrible future to unfold. They are more attentive to the present moment. The only obstacle you have to overcome is your own brain.

Humans naturally have a negative bias, and this is affected by the things that happen to us in our lives. We are way more likely to remember negative events than positive ones because that is our brains' way of keeping us safe. Most of us live in relative safety—we're not being hunted by anything or even having to forage for our food—so the negativity bias only serves to disjoint us from other people. The trauma that other people have possibly caused also affects our negativity bias and changes the way we look at the people whom we might need as part of our lives in order to be our most complete and happy selves. Most of us, after all, are not dreaming of being hermits in the woods and slipping quietly into nothing (but props to you if that's your dream).

Manifestation requires that we address what is holding us back, and take a close look at our negativity bias and how it may be limiting us. Say "thank you" and let go of what you no longer need. You are worthy of your own healing; manifestation happens when you decide you are also worthy of moving forward.

Science

We have a level of awareness about the world around us at all times. This is why some people seem more in tune with the present moment or with very small details in nature; their brain is changing the way they focus and what information they are taking in. In today's world, information comes at us from all directions at all times. Think about driving. You have a passive and necessary amount of information about what is going on behind you and beside you, yet in a way, you are only actively absorbing certain things that are right in front of you. There are appropriate places to direct our attention and advantageous ways to take in stimulation. When you see specks of dust on your windshield while driving, you can be distracted, but seeing the same dust when cleaning your car gives you the chance to get it spotless.

When your brain processes stimulation while you are driving, it is processing it so you are not going to get injured. You're looking out for very specific details that you need to stay safe behind the wheel while ignoring unnecessary and distracting details. When we're out in nature and we hone in on the sound of a rattlesnake rather than the rattling of leaves in wind, it's because our brains are subconsciously searching for those sounds to keep us safe. The law of attraction teaches us to subconsciously search for what we want. Doing so helps us become more attuned to what we are looking for in our lives.

Just as we teach ourselves to look out for people who are texting and drinking a soda while driving, we can also learn to hone in on the things we want to attract, because in reality, we are just seeing what is already there. It is a matter of what we choose to perceive. Everything is already there, so choose what you want to see. We'll be safe—we're already fantastic predictors of the negative.

CHAPTER 2

Where the Magic Begins

Here, you will learn who magic is for, who can do it, and how it can help you on your spiritual path. You will also learn a few exercises that will help establish your connection to the realness of magic as it lives inside of us. Remember that magic is a connection to all; there is no one type of magic, and there is no right or wrong magic.

Offer yourself a nonjudgmental space to read this chapter. There is power in the singularity of you, and this chapter asks you to confront some of the things that are painfully blocking your connection to your universal depth. There is no right or wrong way to explore your depth—that reaching inside is a magic of its own. As you learn to better connect with yourself, you may find that your connection to magic is more powerful. Why? You are magic.

Who Can Do Magic?

Anyone can practice magic. It's not hereditary, and it's not exclusive to a certain community or society. Everyone has access to magic. While the concept of magic is universal and available to everyone, the practices of magic have extreme variables and aren't necessarily open to everyone. Many are divided by faith base, region, and religious beliefs. Magic also requires practice, dedication, and fine-tuning. It might flow easily to some and be harder to practice for others. Magic is instinctual and generally pulls its practitioners through a natural magnetic connection.

The desire to learn magic requires not only self-discovery, but also a thirst for knowledge that will certainly lead you into esoteric and occult topics. Many rites and rituals are open for discovery and can be used in your personal practice. However, some are culturally specific or may require initiation. For example, Wicca is a religion that requires dedication and studying for a full year and a day before being initiated into a Wiccan coven. Santeria, Vodoun, Obeah, Hoodoo, and Brujeria are all culture-specific religions with practices that may not be intended to be practiced by everyone. This book does not encompass all traditions and is specific only to magic and manifestation and is not meant to limit how you practice your craft.

Everyone's magic journey is going to be different and influenced by everything from your culture to your life experiences. There are no two journeys that look alike, and yours deserves the same respect that you offer to others. Your life is already part of your magical practice; now all you have to do is the magic. While it may also seem mundane, learning about different aspects of magic is an important step in the process. Remember, knowledge is power.

It Starts with You

Magic can be messy. It does not have to be aesthetically pleasing, and it is not something you are going to master tomorrow. So, stop scrolling through your Instagram feed and judging your magic based off a shot someone took way more times than a spell takes to set up. That's not magic; that's branding. Your magic is not going to look like someone else's unless you're going out of your way to make it look like that, and that is not honoring what a complete person you are. Take some time to think about what you enjoy the most about magic and your spirituality. What gives you the feeling of euphoria in your practice?

Do not limit yourself. Look at other forms of witchcraft. Perhaps you find that you have a connection to a specific deity. What pantheon are they from? What civilizations have worshipped them? These are key components for customizing your craft.

While learning is a huge part of strengthening your craft, you do not have to adhere to everything that any particular book tells you to do. Your description and practice of your universe is going to be different than mine, and because of that, we can learn new pieces of magic from each other.

Your magical journey is a process of discovering more about you, and part of that self-discovery involves looking at any internal conflicts you may have previously avoided. It's time to take a look. Your most magical self is waiting on the other side of the negative narratives you have created to shield yourself from change. Breaking down the perception of self-denial is a hard and ongoing process, but a necessity as we move though our lives and dive deeper into our spiritual worlds. There are various ways to dive deep into our internal worlds to find our most magical selves.

SELF-AWARENESS

It can be jarring for us to see ourselves as we really are, as more than our thoughts, as a complete person with a colorful set of experiences, yet just like everyone else. Self-awareness is a powerful tool for achieving self-acceptance. Self-awareness can help fine-tune our dreams. Not everyone actually fully knows what they want. Some people live life constantly trying to do what they think other people want them to do. If you have been searching for outside acceptance before you find some semblance of inside acceptance, it's time to turn those eyes to the mirror.

Knowing your faults is important, but it's just as important to recognize all the wonderful things about yourself. Dwelling entirely on what you'd like to change does not do service to the wonderful person that you are. If you find yourself shaping your dreams in service of the acceptance of others, it's time to shape your dreams in service of what actually makes you happy. Maybe external pressure has set you onto a path that you don't necessarily feel right on, but you feel safe from judgment on it. It's time to break free from this obligation to others' desires that you've thrust upon yourself, but breaking free begins by seeing what's there.

You are more than a collection of memories; you are this very moment. Sit in the quiet. This is a time where you are just going to observe the thoughts that come to your mind. Your mind may want to react to these thoughts but try not to. Just see them and let them go. Those thoughts are not you; they're part of the way you process the world, but they don't necessarily make you who you are. Consider what you are doing—if you are standing or sitting in a chair or on the floor. Consider the way your throat fills your neck and how your eyelids rest over your eyes. That is you. If you smile, is your smile small or wide? Who do you think of when you think of a smile? Let that thought float there, don't ask why just yet—simply let your thoughts happen. After you've had this quiet time with yourself, write about your experience. If anything really stuck with you, the writing process is a good time to work out the why. Be open to you; you are the person who deserves your honesty the most.

SELF-ACCEPTANCE & SELF-LOVE

When we practice self-awareness, sometimes we might not like everything we see. That's okay. You likely don't like every little thing about every person you meet. You also probably don't hold people's flaws against them or consider them a bad person for them. So why judge yourself more harshly? Offer yourself grace for the passing thoughts you have or for the insanely high standards you might set for yourself, only to fall short. The internal voice that may make you feel less than likeable is not who you are. And rather than be concerned about how other people think about us, recognize that they probably see us in a similar way to how we see them.

Love and acceptance are what we offer to those we care about, but if we're not caring about ourselves, we cannot offer ourselves love and acceptance. You are worthy of your own love and care. The journey to this realization is yours and yours alone, but oftentimes it requires dismantling a narrative of negativity that no one else even sees in us. Self-acceptance is a path; it's the neutral "I am." Self-love is the journey—the movement toward the path of acceptance, the caretaking moments where you stop the barrage of self-depreciation.

It's time for some mirror work. Self-acceptance can feel slogan-y and detached from reality, but it is only because our reality has been shaped around ladling negativity over ourselves. Pouring positivity over yourself isn't going to feel normal or right at first, but the practice is a type of care. This is a daily exercise.

1 *When you wake up in the morning, say, "Good morning, (your name)!"*

2 *After you get up, make your way to the mirror, look into your eyes, and again say, "Good morning, (your name). I love you, (your name)."*

3 *Smile at yourself, even if you have to make yourself do it and even if it feels unnatural at first.*

If you can do this every day for a month, you're on the right path. Don't give up. If you miss a day, just do it the next one, or do it before bed, too. Good morning and goodnight. Say "I love you" to yourself daily.

SELF-DISCOVERY

Discovery is fun, you are an adventure, and it's time to explore yourself to the fullest. Are you mathematical or creative? Are you a free spirit? Maybe you're someone who loves creature comforts. These are all wonderful things about you, and you are constantly growing; sometimes it may feel challenging to keep up with who you are. We may sometimes even surprise ourselves with new depths that we have just started to access.

Maybe you've suddenly found that you can focus on work better than ever, getting tasks done faster. You might be surprised because you did not think you could do that much before. This is an example of us not offering ourselves the grace of belief that we are capable. This is a type of looking away from our own ability in favor of a negativity that either keeps us where we are or keeps us dependent on someone else.

Self-discovery can be uncomfortable when we realize that we really are more than we give ourselves credit for. Sometimes, we may want to deny ourselves this credit, because that kind of power inevitably brings about change. While change is good and part of life, and you are made of exactly what change is, the idea of change can also be scary for some. The journey of self-discovery leans on self-acceptance and love. While you are discovering yourself, you are also loving yourself.

There is no one way to discover you; just be open and avoid spinning a narrative of negativity just because it feels safe. You're going to be okay; you already have everything you need: you.

*Sometimes, we are not yet experts on ourselves, and that
presents a good opportunity to get to know ourselves.
We are our first best friends, our closest playmates, and
containers of multitudes. Take yourself out on a date. Go
somewhere romantic and natural, like a beach or another
body of water (since water aids in communication). Observe
your inner and outer environment. Write down how you
feel about anything or anyone that catches your attention
and ask why it or they caught your eye. Did it remind you of
something? Or did you just have an experience of something
being completely new? View your notes as though they are
your introduction to another person. What did you like about
the way your date (you) observes the world?*

Why Magic?

Magic links us to the ancients who offer us guidance, our
higher selves, and our loved ones, who may or may not be
living. Magic is communal and personal. We engage every
day with magical forces without realizing it, in the very
same way we can manifest without offering it a name.

Why are you using magic? Is there something that your
heart desires?

Magic helps us ascend from the problems of the mundane and offers us new perspective on the things that already
surround us. Magic is a bounty of universal opportunity. It
deepens our connection to nature—the very nature that we
are from—and it helps us remember that we are flesh and
bone and part of something fantastic.

It should be used when we feel limited and constrained.
It is there to assist us when we feel that there is no hope.

It is also there to celebrate the hope that is to come. Magic can provide us comfort when we feel alone or can offer community when we are together.

Magic is the depth of our spiritual vision; it creates the shadow and light that defines the world that we walk through. It alters our mundane into symbology and ancestral guidance. It creates meaning in the places that seemed to previously have none.

Empathy, in a way, is a type of magic—the magic that we use to connect with one another and ourselves. In a musical, characters break out into song to convey the depths of emotion that a monologue may not necessarily reach, with tone and variation and poetry that may not be natural to speech in the way it is to song. Magic is the song, and you are the actor, so let yourself sing. There is no reason to withhold the emotion that is your magic. It is there and it is speaking to you to convey a message that only you can let out.

So why magic when the world can be explained through tangible and practical sciences?

Magic and science were synonymous for the ancients. We cut ourselves off from that in some way and developed a methodical and critical view of the world. We can offer science the understanding soul of magic when we consider our connection to the universe. Nature and science walk hand in hand; science offers boundaries, while magic offers symbolism. In a way, science offers us the frame to the painting that is the art of magic.

What ideas have held you back from participating in magic? Why did you choose to limit yourself in that way? Magic is not the work of the devil, nor is it held under the sway of any dogmatic constructs. Magic offers liberation to those of us who are on the fringe. So I ask again—why magic? Well, why not?

CHAPTER 3

Manifestation in Practice

Before we jump into the trenches of manifestation and magic, we must first study the basics and master them. This chapter will cover the importance of setting intentions, centering, grounding, and shielding and protection, as well as the use of ritual. Once you master the basics, you will be able to implement them in your day-to-day practice with ease, making your manifestation much more potent. While practitioners should change things up to suit their practice, these basics provide a good foundation. Routine, tradition, and ritual may not sound exciting at first, but they are necessary and have been used for centuries by many accomplished witches, magicians, shamans, and spiritual practitioners. In fact, most spells that we see from antiquity typically require the practitioner to not only be grounded, but to also implement some form of ritual. Read on about these crucial magical tenets to manifest safely with ease.

The Basics

◇◇◇◇◇◇◇◇◇◇◇◇

The practice of manifestation is the art of calling in what you desire, focusing on that desire, and believing it to be so real that indeed it becomes your reality. While the concept itself may seem fairly simple, it is important to remember that everything—especially involving magic—requires preparation and proper planning before execution. The rules may change based on the specific practice you choose to follow, the spell or ritual you've chosen to assist you in your manifestation, and what exactly it is that you wish to manifest.

If you are aligning your special faith to a specific tradition, you may wish to implement the techniques and wisdom of that faith when practicing acts of manifestation. Within the realm of magic and witchcraft, there are typically two types of such practices: "low magic" and "high magic." These are both umbrella terms used to cover a broad range of magical practices.

Low magic refers to any kind of magical practice that does not require the use of ritual or ceremony. The concept of low magic is found predominantly in folk magic, where practitioners use common tools and ingredients in place of prayers, ritual circles, and sacred rites. Also known as practical magic by modern-day practitioners, low magic usually requires nothing more than your will and a handful of materials for the magic to work. Low magic is used primarily for things that are more tangible, personal, and might need to happen quickly. It can be implemented for healing, hexing, financial gain, and attracting love.

High magic, on the other hand, is much more complicated, requiring a certain level of commitment and dedication. For the most part, high magic is useful when goals or desires are a little more intangible and geared toward spiritual enlightenment or a connection to the divine or supernatural. Spirit communication and the connection to deities, spirit guides, angels, demons, etc., usually requires the use of more complex rituals, a magic circle, some form of sacrifice or offering, and the speaking of words and chants. Rituals allow us to truly imbue spellwork with our desires.

When incorporating magic and spellwork into your manifestation practice, it is important to think about your goal and how much effort you think it will take to achieve that goal. The greater the goal, the greater the spellwork should be, and the more energy and magic may be required to achieve it.

In traditional witchcraft, Wicca, and other forms of witchcraft such as folk magic, you will find that many spells and rituals are meant to be performed during certain days, times of the month, and lunar phases. This is tied to the symbolism of the seasons and the planetary hours that play a part in witchcraft. You will also find that many spells might call for obscure items, tools, and ingredients. Substitutions, as well as making necessary and realistic changes, are both okay. If you wish to do a spell right away, but the next full moon isn't for another two weeks, you could compromise by performing it on a Monday, which is Moon's Day. If your spell calls for European mandrake or deadly nightshade (two herbs that are quite difficult to find), you could use rosemary instead. Your practice should not feel rigid; however, sometimes it is necessary to follow the rules, at least until you know how to bend them.

PRACTICING RESPONSIBLY

As mentioned earlier, there is no such thing as white or black magic. Those concepts are racist, outdated, and, if we're being frank, tacky. Nature is neutral, and outside of Abrahamic religions, there isn't much need for the concept of good and evil. Nature simply encourages you to use your common sense. A snake isn't evil just because it bites you; it bites you because you're in its way, or you've hurt or scared it without realizing. So really, nature asks for you to pay attention. And deep listening to the world around you is the first step in truly powerful manifestation. Simply listen and be honest with yourself. Being real is about being planted in reality, acknowledging and moving through its ups and downs with mindfulness. You're worth experiencing that from yourself.

In witchcraft, you are your own judge, jury, and executioner. With that said, if you decide to do something to someone else through spellwork—such as hexing them or attempting to influence their free will—you will face the consequences of your actions. Nature has a funny way of creating balance. The manipulation of nature will always shift back to balance, and you want to make sure that shift back is in your favor. Before you begin a magical practice, ask yourself, "Is it worth it?"

Let's talk about love magic as a perfect (and classical) example of a back and forth of whims and wills. If someone is just not that into you, and you magically force them into a relationship with you, do you really think that relationship will progress or work in either party's favor? No. People who should end up together generally do. To suggest that so-and-so is perfect for you, if only they were in love with you, isn't true and it isn't fair. People have their own will, and that will is a human force of magic. Don't allow yourself to be consumed by the delusion that your magical will is stronger than someone else's, so much so that they'll bend and break for you. Even if they bend at first, they'll eventually snap, and the force of their will could very easily make itself known. What's worse, they could end up an absolute shell of a person, or obsessed with you in the most uncomfortable way possible.

The ultimate takeaway here is to never manifest under the influence of your own ego with no regard for the free will, desires, and boundaries of others. Manifestation is actually a process of self-discovery and brutal self-honesty. Your goals should always make sense. Not everyone is going to be a billionaire like Jeff Bezos either naturally or magically, but you could bring more prosperity and abundance into your life through spellwork to start your own business or live in relative comfort.

Intentions

If you don't know what you want, how are you going to get it? Sometimes, an intention might mean finding that thing you are passionate about before you can start manifesting the process of being more involved in that very passion. While this might be difficult to hear, if your intention is to "make more money" you need to have a *how*. How is a key part of your intention. In fact, if you are setting intentions, you might want to go through the WWWWWH hierarchy: who, what, when, where, why, how. Those are questions that I think of every time I start to create the inkling of a plan, because while some of my plans are wonderful and achievable, others are wildly unrealistic or self-destructive.

In instances where our intentions aren't aligned with reality, or our true desires, we can easily and constructively question our intentions to get a better handle on them before moving forward.

- **Who?** Who is involved in this? Who would you like to be? Who is your ideal self?
- **What?** This might be a hard one. Is it music? Is it sales? Is it a vacation? A homemaking endeavor?
- **When?** Think about how time actually works and set this goal for yourself in a real way. If you're trying to master playing the guitar, it won't happen in one month, but perhaps you will have learned a few chords in that time.
- **Where?** Think about your realistic and magical destination. Where does this lead you? Physically? Spiritually? Emotionally?
- **Why?** This can be a challenging question to ask, as it often prompts us to make changes in our lives, but that is simply part of the process. Questioning the why of your intention doesn't mean you should give up if you encounter some heavy or hurtful truths; it means you should give in to your real needs and wants.
- **How?** Action. Patience. Manifestation.

When it comes to intentions, remember that you're not making a wish. And you're not asking for the intention either. Setting an intention is a statement, a fact that will come to fruition. French astrologer and seer Nostradamus seemed to have it down. By making prophetic predictions and writing them down, he essentially manifested them. Likewise, with manifestation magic, you have to be your own oracle, your own fountain of honesty.

Let's practice an intention I often have to set for myself when studying, pleasure reading, or building furniture: "I will read the whole book and follow the instructions." Wonderful. I absolutely believe that you will, can, and should. You are becoming a manifestation master as you move onward. Keep studying, keep reading, keep manifesting.

Write down your intention on a small piece of paper. Make sure that it is a direct statement. Take the paper in your hands, close your eyes, and visualize what you wish to manifest. Imagine it right in front of you. What does your life look like if you have it? Focus on all the details. Fold the piece of paper three times and imagine that it is a seed. Bury the paper in your backyard, or in a potted plant in your home. As you nurture that plant, you will be nurturing what you wish to manifest. Think about that intention every time you see that plant or tend to your backyard. Imagine your intention blooming like a beautiful flower over time.

Centering

Centering is a necessity in our lives, and something that you may practice regularly without realizing it. The deep breaths you took before delivering a big speech in front of your class as a kid? That's centering. It's finding yourself in the waves of the ocean, and being able to confidently say, "I am right here right now, and all I have to do is row." Finding your center is about bringing all of the energy that is buzzing around your body to your core.

Finding your center is, both in life and in manifestation, pivotal. Centering ourselves can help us swim away from the waves of dissociation that are often felt with issues such as depression, anxiety, and stress. Centering brings us into the now of our bodies. Offering yourself complete access to your energy is a necessity in any sort of spellwork because magic workings take energy.

Think of your core like a battery. It's charging, or draining, as you move through the world. Offer yourself time to discover what gives you energy. What do you draw energy from in your life? It could be anything, like swimming, dancing, sitting still, breathing, or reading. Other activities, like doomscrolling or spending time with certain people, can drain your energy. It's perfectly fine to recognize what does and doesn't give you energy or make you feel good. Especially when it comes to people—family members, friends, lovers, and coworkers—knowing who energizes or drains you allows you to be intentional about how and when you spend time with them and how much energy you offer or expend when doing so.

You can also rely on outside sources, or structured activities, to center yourself. Is there music that makes you feel calm and refreshed? Soothing sounds can be a great way to feel the energy in the core of your body. If it ever feels difficult to get in touch with your core, or challenging to channel your energy in an intentional way, meditating even for few minutes a day can help. Meditation allows you to feel incredibly present in the world around you.

Remember, only you can truly tap into and understand how your energy feels, as it is uniquely a part of you. Energy, and therefore the methods of centering, are different for everyone. Your special and diverse energies are not going to feel exactly like other people may describe their own. When centering, the goal is not to feel like someone else, or even feel something wildly different than usual.

Rather, you're tuning into the world and into your body, and accessing your greater ability to manifest your personal magic.

Find a private, comfortable, and quiet place in your house that it is free of clutter. If this is your bedroom, you may wish to find a space on the floor, or in the center of your bed. Lie down and place your left hand over your stomach. Breathe in through your nose and out through your mouth. As you take a deep breath in, feel your stomach rise against your hand. When you exhale, give your stomach a slight push. Your shoulders, chest and neck should not move as you breathe. As you get more comfortable and into your breathing routine, try to imagine pulling all the energy from the different parts of your body into the center of your heart/chest area. You can do this by simply visualizing light emitting from your chest. Next, imagine that your heart is a battery and is charged by pulling energy from different parts of your body, such as the tips of your fingers, your toes, your head etc. The more you charge your center, the more centered you become. Perform this exercise whenever you are about to do an important task such as public speaking, performing, or participating in a social event or sport.

Grounding

To ground oneself is to set foot in reality. It helps us remember that we are very real and worthy of recognizing our place in this world. That doesn't mean the earthly world is not inherently magical—life is magic—and we must recognize the divine magic of our lives in acts like eating, bathing, and stretching. Those are all aspects of grounding. Grounding is a rejuvenating celebration of the event that is your existence. It connects us to the element of earth and makes us feel protected and stable. A connection to the physical world can bring us joy, and offers a view of our current abundance, allowing us to see with greater clarity the possible doorways to even more abundance. There are a lot of ways to practice grounding, but one of my personal favorites is an intentional indulgence, such as enjoying cake and ale. In the best way, rituals can drain your energy, and offering yourself nourishment that your body both needs and deserves gives you a moment to rejoice, rather than sinking into the lull of tired discontentment.

Some people decide that they must always be in the astral plane and use their incredibly vivid imaginations to keep themselves ungrounded. Some people crave so much to be spiritually attuned or gifted that they will do anything, like convincing themselves that they are guided by the spirit of Tutankhamun's wet nurse while wearing a muumuu and enough crystals to fill a three-foot-deep swimming pool. Some may be so ungrounded as to be easily coaxed into ideologies that can be dangerous for them and the world around them. Remaining grounded in the mundane world allows us to make the most of our here and now. While reincarnation is a real possibility, we should offer this life the respect it deserves by being present in it whenever possible and exploring our spiritual world when we feel safe and ready to connect.

Find a quiet space where you can be alone. Sit in a chair and place your feet firmly on the ground. (You may wish to do this without socks or shoes on.) Close your eyes and take a few deep breaths, breathing in through your nose and out through your mouth. After you take a few moments to focus on your breathing, close your eyes and imagine that you're being pulled down to the ground by a giant magnetic force. Beginning at your feet, imagine that a ball of white light is traveling up through your feet to your knees, to your pelvis, up through your chest, through your neck, and to the base of your skull. As you visualize this white light moving through you, imagine yourself becoming more stable, as if you are a tree and your feet are roots connecting you to the earth. When you're visualizing the white light at the base of your skull, imagine that you are being pulled through your head by a string extending into the heavens. As you feel this pull, let your posture straighten. Imagine that you are being pulled in opposite directions—into the heavens above and into the earth below. As they say in magic, witchcraft, and the occult: "As above, so below."

Shielding

It's raining heavily outside, and while you may need to go out to get your day started, you don't want to get soaked and catch a cold. There's an umbrella right by the door. You're going to use that umbrella, right? Why wouldn't you? Shielding magically is very similar to using an umbrella on a rainy day. The umbrella protects you from the rain, just as shielding offers protection from other aspects of your reality. Peace can be difficult to find at times, and shielding can defend us from negative thoughts. While you may have very real things to worry about, worrying isn't going to help you move forward in a productive way. When you're trying to go to sleep, does worrying about something that might happen under a specific but imagined set of circumstances actually help you accomplish your goal of falling asleep?

Our brains are quite busy every moment of every day, alerting us to potential dangers. But they don't always act as our best friends when it comes to filtering out negative thoughts or practices. Knowing this, you can offer your brain some tools to continue to help keep you safe but also recognize thoughts, feelings, and practices that are *not* actually going to harm you. Shielding practices can quiet the hustle and bustle of a mind at work to better protect you. Shielding gives your mind the opportunity to defend itself without paying any real mind to the complicated series of messages about some imagined doom that try to come in.

Those negative spirits, feelings, and energies that are hanging onto you can be warded off with your practice of shielding, and your mind will thank you. It is much easier to focus when you are not under spiritual attack. We should remember that when something is out of our control and nonphysical, it is not actually in control of us.

Offering yourself protection is the best thing you can do if you feel that you are blocked by fear or unsure of what you truly desire. Feeling safe puts you in a state of readiness for your manifestation magic. Your feelings are going to manifest a reality, and if your feelings are latched onto unhelpful things happening around you—real or imagined—those energies might draw you to it. It's okay to feel nervous before manifestation, to anticipate some negative thoughts, but you must keep in mind that these things are far less factual than the statement of your magical manifestation. You are not a car accident waiting to happen, you are not going to fall down a flight of stairs, you are not going to get possessed, your best friend/partner is not going to betray you simply because you are trying to manifest good into your life. Shielding is the intentional act of telling yourself that you're manifesting protection into your reality. The more you offer yourself the manifestation of protection, the easier the manifestation of other ideas may be.

Before you dive into this shielding exercise, think about what you want to manifest. How important is it to you? Is this something that you absolutely want to bring to fruition? With your manifestation clear in your mind, imagine all the outside forces that can affect you and distract you from achieving your goal. Now imagine a circle of blue light surrounding you, creating a barrier around you, physically separating you from the outside world. This is also known as casting a circle. You can use your pointer finger and "draw" a circle in the air around you, envisioning blue light emitting from your fingertips as you create the circle. When casting the circle, vocalize that you wish to cast out any negative influences, spirits, and distractions. Call on any spirit guides, deities, or ancestors with whom you work, and invite them into the circle to assist you with your manifestation practice. Invest in a hematite ring, or another hematite piece of jewelry, to aid in shielding and protecting you from outside influences that may interfere with your manifestation.

Divination

Divination is an absolute must before attempting to manifest. It allows you the opportunity to check in with yourself and objectively determine if what you wish to manifest is actually possible. Divination itself is the practice of seeking knowledge through the use of intuition, communication, psychic abilities, guidance from spirit guides and deities, and magical tools. For centuries, divination has been a key component for how people make decisions, whether it be a king seeking advice prior to battle, a farmer asking for insight about the future of his crops, or the youth wanting to know the prospects of a relationship with the person they are courting. There are many forms of divination that can assist you in finding out whether or not your desire is achievable and worth pursuing. Think of divination as the tool that will give you the green light or confirmation you need to delve into the workings necessary to manifest your desires.

Tarot cards are a great starting point. Tarot is a fixed system, thereby offering a clear and definite answer to the questions you propose. A pendulum is another tool that is perfectly suitable for gaining answers to questions about the outcome of your manifestation. Incorporating divination into your magical and manifestation practices is necessary and will assist you in fine-tuning that which you are bringing into reality. If you receive no response at all, or a hint of a negative outcome, trust the finding of the divination and rethink that which you want to manifest. *Is it realistic? Is it something I should wait on? Is it worth putting all my energy into?* If divination about your manifestation offers up omens, obstacles, or warnings, pause to think through your intended manifestation. You may also use divination to ask for guidance on how to achieve your goal. Perhaps you don't need any magic after all. Through divination, you may find out that all you need to do is talk to a specific person, or wait for a specific amount of time, before you get what you want.

Divination is not only used for gaining wisdom about your manifestation practices. It can also be used to seek out information about future events, relationships, career opportunities, and spiritual affairs. When performing divination, think about how you're taking part in a practice that has been used for thousands of years, by many different civilizations.

The magic does not reside in the tarot deck or other tools you use to perform the divination; the magic resides in you. There are many different forms of divination, some very obscure and others more well known. Do you connect with tarot cards? If not, try the pendulum. If pendulums aren't your thing, look into dice.

Lean into exploring the different types of divination to see which one may offer you proper guidance. You may find that you're attracted to multiple forms and tools. Feel free to explore them. Don't be surprised if you end up combining practices as you become more acquainted with divination. Many practitioners use multiple tools during one divination session or reading. Do what works best for you.

Ritual

◇◇◇◇◇◇◇◇◇◇◇◇◇

Ritual is a practice or custom that is performed in a sacred way. Typically, it is done in routine, similar to a tradition. A ritual is a way of causing energetic movement that will allow you to get into the flow, pushing you toward your manifestation goals. Not all rituals are the same, and there may be different rituals that you perform for different workings and spells. Rituals vary from practice to practice, depending on the religion or faith to which you subscribe. While there is no right or wrong way to perform a ritual, there definitely are rules and guidelines that should be taken into account.

Some aspects of manifestation may not require a ritual. If you are performing low magic, such as creating a charm, talisman, or amulet, you may not need to do a ritual beforehand. Rituals are typically performed on specific days that are sacred to specific faiths. Rituals may also be performed over the course of several days. For example, February 13th through the 15th is Lupercalia, an ancient Roman holiday celebrating fertility, renewal, and love. Rituals and spells centered around love, sex, and fertility would be executed during those days.

Rituals can be incorporated into your day-to-day life to enhance your magical practice. Rituals do not have to be long or drawn out; they can be as simple as taking a shower or lighting incense. As you grow in your practice, you'll eventually pick up different methods of performing rituals that may become part of your personal tradition. A shower or ritual bath, for instance, is great for cleansing before any spiritual or magical act. In Hellenic witchcraft, bathing was a way of clearing oneself from "miasma" (me-ahz-mah), the static energy that makes us mortal. By cleansing ourselves ritualistically, we are making ourselves spiritually pure and worthy of the divine. That cleansing removes the mundane energies that may infiltrate and psychically pollute our bodies, affecting us emotionally, mentally, and spiritually. Water itself is very magical, not only as a conduit to the other realm, but also as a remover of impurities.

Following a good cleansing, choose attire that is specifically set aside and used solely for ritual. This can be a robe or cloak or an oversized white T-shirt and silk pajama bottoms. You stay most connected during ritual when you feel the most comfortable. Continuing with the cleansing process, clear your space with incense that has both cleansing and protective qualities, feeling free to combine for their properties. Some useful pairings are frankincense and myrrh, rose and dragon's blood, and sage and sweet grass. Many witches keep an altar, a sacred space. Rituals can consist of giving offerings to the ancestors, deities, and spirit guides with whom you work. If a ritual is simply for spiritual connection, and not with the intention of performing magic, dedicate time during the ritual to meditation. Ending rituals by thanking the elements, guides, deities, ancestors, and spirits, and changing out of your designated ritual attire, provides a positive boundary between the ritual and the rest of your life.

After the Practice

Following a spell or ritual, you may feel low in energy. Waiting for the results of your magical workings can leave us feeling impatient. Now, it's time to take care of yourself. Eat a delightful treat, being mindful as you do to allow it to ground you. Take a relaxing bath, light a candle, or use a selenite wand to take a moment to cleanse your energy. This is about rewarding yourself for the work you've done for yourself. Making sure you feel deserving of the real and practical care that your body and mind need is an absolute necessity and still part of manifestation. Your body is your first point of contact for everything, physical and spiritual. Be kind to it, nourish it, and return to the exercises about kindness and self-love.

Manifestation is a process. Remember what we said about having realistic goals? Now is the time to think of your manifestation as practical as well. Write out what you can do to practically move toward your dreams. Take music as an example: If your manifestation is musically related, make sure you set aside time to practice your instrument, seek feedback from others, and continue to learn. If your manifestation concerns finding a new place to live, check out listings, gather quotes, plan your budget, etc.

Do not be discouraged by the scale or loftiness of your goals. Write down your main manifestation goal and branch it out into smaller, more digestible steps that will ultimately get you there. It might look like a lot on paper, but as you move forward, some of these things just have a way of working themselves out, and you'll be surprised by how easy some of the others are. If you're seeking love, why don't you download a dating app and make the first move? You might encounter rejection here and there, but think of being rejected as a step up, a clearing out of the people and things that are not the best options—the removal of the unnecessary paves the way for the arrival of what is in your best interest.

Keep your eyes open; the universe is always trying to communicate with you. What numbers stand out to you? Have you been seeing unusual animals lately? Maybe you've been hearing bells or a certain type of music in public more than before. Some things are warnings, telling us to avoid certain paths and places, or even people. Pay attention to those gut feelings that are absolutely signs of what is happening. Trust in your own intuition. Write down the signs—the events that seem to occur around you at an unusual rate—as the universe is trying to say some- thing. Take time to journal how you feel about these signs, as new insights may arise.

What happens when manifestation works? What if it is something that needs upkeep? Manifestation magic is part of the ongoing process of being involved in the magic of your life. You can shield and protect the beautiful life you are creating through continued rituals of protection manifestation. You can set new goals for yourself, and you can help the people you love on their paths to manifestation by offering to practice with them. Sometimes, giving other people practical and magical tools is a wonderful way to keep our own practice while also building a community of powerful manifestors. Performing manifestation maintenance also allows us time to meaningfully check in on our goals, desires, and feelings. You are a force of manifestation. Remember that.

CHAPTER 4

Methods of Manifesting

The time has come to delve into the mysteries of manifestation and magic—to unfold arcane knowledge and discover the different methods and practices of magic, witchcraft, and manifestation. In this chapter, you will learn the different aspects of the craft, as well as the techniques and tools used by witches and magical practitioners alike. The methods and techniques you will read about in these pages come from a culmination of varied practices and rituals that were either recorded many centuries ago or passed down orally throughout the years. Despite having origins in certain cultures, a lot of these practices overlap and synchronize with other practices and faiths; the practice and belief in magic resonates throughout all cultures. Although magical methods might have their own unique names, they are often rooted in the same fundamental concepts, which tether us all, witches and nonwitches, to the collective conscious.

Methods

◇◇◇◇◇◇◇◇◇◇◇◇◇

It's time to learn about manifestation's connection to witchcraft and magic. The majority of magical practices, rituals, spells and rites used in witchcraft involve the use of tools, some of which can be used individually or in conjunction with another practice. For example, you may use a pendulum to assist in picking out tarot cards for a specific question that was asked. Depending on the practice and the practitioner, casting a sacred circle before performing a spell may feel like a necessity. In both examples, the practitioner is performing a ritual prior to performing another act of magic, but each act benefits the other.

As you grow in your own practice, you will find what works best for you. It is important to learn as much as you can about each individual practice before incorporating it in your personal craft or combining it with another practice. As you do your research and discover connections to practices and tools that feel most natural to you, you will also find that certain practices and rituals may not feel right. Never force yourself to connect to all of the methods described in this book if they do not speak to you. The real goal is to develop your skills with however many methods speak to you and master those for present and future use. It is far better to be fully connected to a few methods, arts, and skills than to halfheartedly approach all of them simply because you feel obligated. Remember, your craft is your own. The practices listed in the next few pages are those that are most commonly used in the practice of witchcraft.

SIGILS

Sigils, symbols that are either painted or inscribed, have been used for a millennium. A popular concept used in ceremonial magic, sigils were revived during the 19th- and 20th-century occult movements, and brought to the forefront by English occultist and ceremonial magician Aleister Crowley. During medieval times, sigils were used to summon demons. They are symbols of magic and power specifically made for and by the practitioner. These symbols are unique and always crafted for a specific purpose. They are intricately designed with a desired manifestation in mind.

One method of using sigils involves writing out what you wish to manifest, such as "I WILL BUY A HOUSE," and then crossing out all the vowels and double letters in the statement. The last step is to then combine the remaining letters, as you see fit, into an image, glyph, or symbol. Thus, you will have created your own custom sigil for the manifestation at hand.

Sigils can be drawn on parchment with ink, written in the air with a wand or ritual blade, drawn with chalk on the ground outside or a wooden floor indoors, or sketched on a piece of paper and concealed in a pocket or shoe. Sigils typically need to be charged and released to fully function. To charge a sigil, place both hands over it, close your eyes, and visualize it in your mind's eye. With your hands over the physical sigil, imagine infusing it with the energy coming from your hands, feeling the heat transferring from your hands. Once a sigil is charged, it is time to release it. This can be done simply by destroying it by burning it, tearing it up, or plunging it into water. To destroy is to activate, and thereby create.

Aside from sigils, which can be thought of as personal seals with intent specific to the practitioner, the use of sacred symbols in magical practices is also useful. Think the Egyptian ankh and eye of Horus, or the lucky horseshoe and four-leaf clover. Such symbols are found throughout various cultures and ancient civilizations, and can represent anything from protection to fertility to wealth. Common sacred symbols that are used today are imbued with centuries of age-old magic and have been used in spellwork or worn as talismans and amulets for millennia. Even the cross, most often associated with crucifixion, is a symbol of protection. Many everyday symbols possess a magical history.

ALTARS

The creation, use, and act of tending to an altar can be an incredibly meditative and empowering part of any magical practice. The altar plays a significant role in witchcraft today, one that derives from the ancient use of the altar in Paganism as a place to practice your witchcraft and magic. Altars, like other tools and customs in witchcraft, are historically and presently found in countless cultures across the world, such as Paganism, Buddhism, Hinduism, and Judeo-Christian places of worship.

Altars are typically a table space solely dedicated to offerings or spiritual workings. Think of the altar as a physical manifestation of your sacred space. It provides a special space to leave your ritual offerings and connect with deities and ancestors. You may find as you grow in your practice that it is best to keep separate altars, such as an altar for connecting with your ancestors, another altar for connecting with deities with whom you work, and yet another altar for the creation of your spells. All altars allow you to separate and focus on your magical workings with intent. Keep in mind that altars do not have to be permanent spaces or setups. You may set up a temporary altar for a specific holiday or celebration, or perhaps for a specific deity you are calling in to assist in timely spellwork.

CANDLE MAGIC

I adore candle magic so much that I wrote an entire book on the subject—*Candle Magic for Beginners: Spells for Prosperity, Love, Abundance, and More*. Candle magic falls under the category of low magic and is one of the simplest forms of witchcraft. It is also one of the easiest methods of manifesting what it is that you want. Plus, it can be a simple and discreet way to work your magic.

In candle magic, the candle serves as the offering, while the flame sends your intention outward into the universe. Using specific colors and types of candles, etching words into the wax, and rubbing essential oil into candles before burning can all serve specific purposes. When selecting the size, the color, and the shape of your candle, as well as the spell you wish to cast, you are taking important steps in the manifestation process.

While candles have become a staple in modern witchcraft, their spiritual origins have roots in Judaism and Catholicism, which may be appealing to those practitioners who come from a religious background. Those who have a difficult time with visualization may find that working with candles is a much easier and more accessible approach to manifesting, as they are tangible tools that can be used to represent what is not yet in this physical reality.

CLEANSING

Cleansing and warding (protection) are incredibly important and influential magical methods. When practicing magic and witchcraft, you are vulnerable to outside forces, whether they be supernatural or not. Magic casts a beacon that attracts outside forces of all kinds.

Cleansing is done through the use of spiritual fumigation, such as the burning of herbs or incense, or more mundane cleaning acts like sweeping. Don't be turned off by the notion of actual cleaning, as there is magic in that act whether you know it or not. For centuries, brooms have been ritualistically used for cleansing negative spaces and offering users protection.

After you cleanse, you must also protect. Whether it be the space that you are working in, or your physical or mental state, protection can be achieved by placing crystals—preferably onyx, black tourmaline, hematite, obsidian, or jet—in the corners of the room, on the windowsills, or above the lip of a door. Salt is another wonderful tool for protection that is easy to come by and super potent: it absorbs and dries out stagnant energy, and wards against and neutralizes negative spirits and malefic workings. Sprinkle salt across your threshold to protect and keep out unwanted vibes, people, and spirits, or use selenite, a salt-based crystal, for charging other crystals and cleansing your ritual tools. You can also carry packets of salt in your pocket for protection.

MEDITATION

Meditation plays a key role in many spiritual practices around the globe. In an earlier chapter, we learned a basic meditation technique, but how does the practice actually assist us with magic and manifestation? When we meditate, we are able to clear from our minds any outside chatter or interfering thoughts, allowing us to focus on our goals and desires.

It is often best and most effective to meditate right before bed, or right upon waking; this allows you to focus on yourself before a day of outside influences begins or after a day of distractions and worries ends. Meditation is important for witches because it not only connects them with their higher selves, but it also allows them a few brief moments to check in with their feelings and emotions, and regain the spiritual connection that sometimes comes untethered during interactions with other people. As you progress in your practice, you will very likely find that you can enhance your manifestation skills by meditation only.

When meditating, imagine what it is that you want to manifest in your mind's eye, and keep this image fixed and focused as you do breathwork. As you advance in the practice, you may also wish to repeat what you desire, much like a mantra. For example, if you're aiming to buy a house, you can repeat the phrase, "I'll buy a house, a house, a house." Say it however many times feels best. This simple repetitive phrase is a basic form of manifestation *and* spellwork. Words have power.

SPIRIT WORK

Whether you realize it or not, we all connect with spirits on a daily basis. While not all witches and magical practitioners specifically work with the spirit realm, it can be quite helpful for all practitioners to tap in and get assistance from that realm.

First, let us address what spirits are. They are not only the souls of the deceased. They reside in almost everything found in nature; this is a concept and belief system known as animism. The belief that everything has a spirit—from animals to the flame of a candle to a flowing river—is most commonly believed amongst Native American cultures and traditions, in Neo-Paganism, and religions such as Vodoun and Santeria.

Because animism posits that all things possess spirits—animals, flora, fauna, and everything in between have the ability to assist in various types of magic. If you are dealing with personal or family matters, ancestral spirits may be able to assist you. If you are looking for financial stability, you may call upon an earth spirit or deity.

You can communicate with spirits using tools for divination such as tarot cards, spirit boards, or pendulums; they may communicate with us through signs and omens as well. The signs and omens that spirits send you will not all appear in a supernatural setting or experience—no need to anticipate flickering lights or rolling fog when you receive a message from spirit. Signs typically appear in our everyday life and can show up in very mundane ways. Noticing the clock has stopped at double numbers such as 11:11 (also known as angel numbers), catching specific song lyrics on the radio that resonate with you, or getting a meaningful message from a fortune cookie are all examples of ways that spirits may be communicating with you.

You can enhance your spirit communication skills by learning different forms of divination, or by simply becoming aware of the signs you are receiving. If you find that you are receiving signs from spirits, this may be the perfect time to set up an altar to leave offerings and other forms of acknowledgment that will enhance your connection to the spirit realm. When you feel that you have established a bond or connection, you may invite the spirits into your circle or sacred space and use their energy to assist with your manifestation.

Preparations

We've made it to arguably one of the most thrilling parts of the craft—hands-on working. Witchcraft is unique amongst other spiritual practices in that witches get to influence and conjure up their own outcomes rather than relying on hope, luck, or the help of others. Witches rely on their natural instincts, talents, and gifts in conjunction with tools provided by nature to conjure up that which they want. A witch does not need to submit to dogmatic religions, or rely upon other beings, to get what they want; they can summon what they want as long as they maintain a balance of nature.

As you start a practice, you must remember a few things. First, treat any tools and ingredients with great respect, especially if the items are from nature (e.g., a crystal), botanical (e.g., fresh herbs), or zoological (e.g., a rabbit's foot). Learning the history and usage of each tool and ingredient in your practice is essential. Having an understanding of the folklore behind the items and ingredients you are using will not only enhance your practice and skill, but further connect you to the energy that resides within that ingredient or tool as well. For example, rosemary may seem like a basic kitchen ingredient, but for thousands of years, it has been used for protection, as well as a prime substitution for other magical herbs or ingredients in spellwork.

From knowing that which you wish to manifest to gathering your tools to learning the history behind them, preparation is always necessary—and essential—in spellwork and witchcraft. Following, you'll find an overview of a few magical necessities that a witch should always aim to have on hand. Typically crafted by the witch themselves, they can be created in conjunction with specific spells, with an intention in mind, or purely to have on hand. If you've managed to create a very effective money-drawing oil, why not create a larger batch for any and all future workings? What's more, the act of making amulets, talismans, oils, candles, charms, etc. can be quite a soothing process, allowing a witch to enter a relaxed and meditative state while preparing for future spellwork.

OILS/BOTANICALS

Botanicals are extremely useful in witchcraft. The intimate relationship between witchcraft and botanicals has a rich and complicated history. Circa the 1500s, herbs were used to ease labor pain, but because it was believed by many from the religious text *Genesis* that labor pains were Eve's punishment from God for her "sins," the medicinal use of herbs and other botanicals were considered the work of the devil. Of the nearly 200 people accused of witchcraft in Salem in 1692, 22 were identified as midwives or healers.

Today, as it was then, the simplest way to make an herbal infusion is by soaking an herb of your choice in olive oil in an airtight container and storing it in a cool, dark area, such as a cabinet, for a week or two. With this method, you can easily make as many herbal oils as you like, either using single herbs or combining herbs. These natural concoctions are great to have on hand at any time, so you are always prepared for spellwork that requires such an oil. You can also begin building your witch's apothecary with some easy-to-find herbs such as poppy seeds, basil, lavender, and thyme. Honey and salt are two others that are great to stock up on, as many spells call on those ingredients.

CHARMS & GRIS-GRIS BAGS

An excellent addition to a witch's arsenal is a handful of charm bags. These bags are typically filled with herbs, crystals, and other curios infused with specific intentions, such as protection, prosperity, or love. The simplest way to make a charm bag is to take a small (approximately 4-by-4-inch) square piece of cloth or felt, and place the desired herbs and curios that relate to your needs in the middle. Then pull the ends of the square upward and toward each other, and tie them in the middle with a piece of cord. This will secure the contents in place and create a ball-like shape. Alternatively, you can place the gathered herbs and curios in a small drawstring bag. Keep in mind that just as with candle magic, the colors and herbs you choose will have different associations. Be sure to reference the color and herb correspondences provided in this book (see pages 145 through 147) to assist you in creating the perfect charm bag. You may wish to make an assortment of different bags to have on hand for different occasions.

Similar to a charm bag, a gris-gris bag also contains herbs, crystals, and curios designated for protection and other magical uses. The gris-gris bag, however, has origins that date back to the Yoruba word *juju*, meaning "fetish," referring to an object containing magical powers or imbued with magic. Gris-gris bags are popular amongst Vodoun and Hoodoo practitioners, and can be found throughout Louisiana, and in Haiti and Africa.

SWEET JARS

No witch can ever have too many jars, especially sweet jars. A sweet jar is one of the easiest forms of spellwork and very enjoyable to make. The concept is simple: make someone sweet on you or sweeten someone up so that you can get what you want from them. Contrary to popular belief, sweet jars are not only for love. Perhaps sweetening up your boss may make them more approachable so that you can ask for a promotion. Sweet jars can also be used to mend conflicts with a friend or help you get a callback for an audition or job interview.

While there are many different ways to create a sweet jar, the basic concept involves a regular- or large-mouth mason jar. You can write either the full name or the initials of the person you wish to sweeten up on a small piece of paper. If you know their astrological sign or birthday, you can add that to the paper for extra measure, along with what it is you wish to get from them. Fold the paper three times toward you, drop it in the mason jar, and then pour honey (pancake syrup will also do) over the paper, fully submerging it. Specific herbs can also be added to enhance the sweetening of the spell. Once the mason jar is sealed, imagine what it is you wish to accomplish and shake the jar vigorously, visualizing that with each shake, the person of your choosing feels more favorably toward you. To round out a sweet jar spell, burn a candle on top of the jar or keep it around your person, shaking it when you need to experience the benefits of that magical sweetness.

AMULETS & TALISMANS

We all wear symbols of power every day without even noticing it—from cross necklaces to evil eye bracelets. Symbols such as these carry a long history of folklore and magic. The symbol of the winged staff with intertwined snakes, commonly seen on hospitals and medical buildings, is actually the caduceus, the staff of Hermes, and an ancient symbol of logistics. In the United States, the caduceus is used as a medical symbol because it was mistaken for the rod of Asclepius—which features a single snake, represents medicine, and belongs to the Greek god of healing.

To discover and invest in amulets and talismans that can enhance your magical workings and manifestations, invest in a reputable book on symbols and symbolism, such as *The Element Encyclopedia of Secret Signs and Symbols: The Ultimate A–Z Guide from Alchemy to the Zodiac,* by Adele Nozedar. Once you research symbolism associated with your desired manifestation, you can easily stock up on symbolic charms by visiting your local craft store's jewelry-making section. Common charms such as eyes, bells, and animal shapes all have magical functions and purposes, and can be tied to charm bags, used in spell jars, or worn as amulets and talismans. If you desire luck and wish fulfillment, for example, you could carry with you, or wear on your person, a wishbone charm. Find your tokens of power and wear them with pride.

FETISHES & POPPETS

The use of poppets and dolls in magic and witchcraft can be found throughout the world and traced far back in numerous civilizations. But of all the tools in a witch's arsenal, poppets and fetishes are probably the most misunderstood. There has long been a stereotype perpetuated that witches craft dolls in the likeness of a person to cause them harm. This harmful use of dolls is especially assumed about practitioners of "black magic" and Voodoo; however, this is merely colonialist propaganda based on racial stereotypes. A fetish, as mentioned earlier, is a figure that has been charged with magical properties, similar to a talisman or amulet, with the difference being that sometimes a fetish can embody a spirit. Fetishes are common tools amongst those who believe in animism. The image of the spirit in the magic mirror of the evil queen in Disney's *Snow White* is a very extreme but still appropriate example of a fetish.

A poppet is a doll usually but not always made of cloth. It is sometimes dressed and crafted to look like a specific person that a witch intends to do a working on. The poppet is named, fed, blessed, and charged. As with the practice of sympathetic magic, or the idea that like affects like, tending to the poppet can enhance the person's desire for them, heal the person, or depending on the practitioner, hinder them. A simple poppet can be made from scrap pieces of cloth or an old T-shirt. You can either cut out the shape of a person and stitch it together, filling it with herbs and cotton stuffing, or you can make a rag doll version. Like sweet jars, poppets are also good to have on hand when you wish to give someone an extra little push, or have a friend or family member who needs healing.

PSYCHIC WORK

What do you think of when you hear the word "psychic"? Unfortunately, the word can carry more negative stigma than the word "witch." When some people think of psychics, they think of charlatans and scam artists. While there are many people out there who do scam people, there are also many with genuine psychic abilities. "Psychic" is an umbrella descriptor that covers a multitude of various categories and gifts.

A psychic is someone who has heightened senses and is more attuned to the world. While some people may have multiple gifts, others gravitate to, or have a stronger connection to, just one. Let me introduce you to what I like to call the clares—people with heightened psychic and intuitive gifts that trigger and vibrate a specific sense. Clairvoyants can receive visions or premonitions that typically have to do with the future. Clairaudients can hear messages. Clairesentients receive messages by touch. Claircognizant people have a clear and distinct way of knowing things that they otherwise would have no reason to know. Clairgustances are able to taste things that aren't physically there, like a favorite childhood candy. Clairaliences' insight comes from smell. The last two clares are more commonly found in those who perform mediumship, spirit work, or necromancy.

While everyone may have some psychic capabilities, not everyone may be as attuned to them. When you do feel attuned to your gifts, you may find that some gifts work in tandem with others. The many different clares, for example, do not necessarily work alone. It's possible you've experienced one or more of these gifts. Maybe you caught a glimpse of something in the house or heard something just as you were drifting off to sleep.

As Paul Huson said in his book *Mastering Witchcraft,* "the moment that you set foot up on the path of witchcraft, a call rings out of the unseen world announcing your arrival." While not all witches consider themselves psychic or use psychic abilities, many who practice witchcraft perform some sort of divination, use intuition, or work with spirits. All of these practices fall under the "psychic" umbrella. As you become more comfortable with the practice of witchcraft, you'll find that the supernatural realm will pull you toward it more and more. Your intuition will eventually peak, and you will find messages all around you.

A good way to enhance your intuition is by using an oracle card deck. Unlike the fixed system of tarot cards, oracle cards allow you to lean into your instincts. What is the card telling you? What does that card reveal about the question you asked? Take a deep breath and explore the various answers that bubble up inside of you. Journal the cards that you pulled, the questions you asked, and the answers you received, so that you can reflect on them later. Keep note of any changes that occur, as this will help you discern fact from fiction, as well as confirm your abilities.

Magical Deities

While not all witches work with the deities, there are many that do. Deities are more than just omnipotent beings that reside up above our world—they are the very archetypes we see ourselves in, and the archetypes we must invoke for certain magical work. As ancient guides, they are a manifestation of mankind's connection to earth and the supernatural.

Working with deities will not only enhance your magic and assist with your manifestation, but also help connect you to your higher self and gain spiritual insight. There are a countless number of deities, many with known origin stories, associated cults, and traditions of worship. With this in mind, don't be surprised if you find contradictory information about a singular deity while conducting research. Know that there is no one right way to work with a deity. And above all, do not feel pressured by other practitioners to work with deities any which way. If connecting and working with spirits and deities is something you wish to explore, Judika Illes's book *Encyclopedia of Spirits* is a good place to begin.

The following list of deities and their magical associations may be helpful for your practice. This list represents a tiny fraction of the vast number of deities associated with magic across the globe. The more you learn about the deities that appeal to you, the more you will connect with them. Also, keep in mind that a connection to a deity may not always come to you as visual manifestations. The goddess Diana, for example, may not appear to you in full figure when you call to her, but you may find that you are seeing cats more frequently, or coming across images of deer and dogs, the very animals that are sacred to her. One way or another, deities make themselves known.

Hecate/Hekate: The Greek goddess of the crossroads, witchcraft, the moon, and necromancy, she's a popular goddess amongst witches and helpful in assisting in spellwork and rituals, as well as deepening your craft.

Isis/Auset: The ancient Egyptian goddess of magic, motherhood, and protection, she is known as the goddess of 10,000 names, and has been synchronized with countless other goddesses.

Thoth: The ancient Egyptian deity of magic, wisdom, and the moon, he is also associated with the Greeks' Hermes, and can assist in creating spells, writing, and formulating manifestations.

Diana: A Roman lunar goddess who is also known as the mother of the witches in Italian witchcraft (Stregheria), she is often associated with the Greek goddess Artemis and is the sister of Apollo. Diana can assist in lunar magic, as well as workings of protection, fertility, and childbirth.

Ceridwen/Cerridwen: A Celtic enchantress and goddess of poetry, Ceridwen is beneficial in assisting with all creative endeavors, and can be invoked in spells for renewal and change.

Circe: The Greek goddess of magic, Circe is known in antiquity as the first witch. In some myths, she is the daughter of Hecate, while in others, her father is the sun god, Helios. Call on her when you wish to enhance your botanical skills or work with herbs and glamor magic.

Pasiphaë: Sister to Circe, mother of the Minotaur, and minor goddess of oracles and divination, she is useful in justice spells and divination.

Heka: The ancient Egyptian word for magic, as well as magic personified, Heka can assist with all types of magic because Heka is Magic. Heka is also a deity of healing, as magic and medicine were one and the same to the ancient Egyptians.

Bucca: Known as the father of witches in traditional witchcraft, he has also been called Pan, Puck, and Poucka. He is also associated with the Celtic Cernunnos and Herne. Call on him to strengthen your skill in witchcraft and deepen your connection to earth and nature.

Tarot

Tarot cards, particularly the major arcana, have long captivated the imagination of witches and nonwitches alike. The cards begin with *le mat* (also known as "The Fool" in modern variations), who is naive and care-free, venturing out into the world with the highest of hopes. It ends with *le monde* ("The World"), which traditionally portrays a woman dancing in a wreath, surrounded by four beings representing the four essential elements of creation (i.e., earth, air, water, and fire); it is a card of completeness and being at one with the cosmos.

In 1909, the Rider Company published what is probably the most commonly used and recognized tarot deck in existence. The majority of magical practitioners are familiar with the artwork of Pamela Colman Smith, the illustrator of the widely used Rider-Waite tarot deck. She followed the magical guidance of famed occultist A. E. Waite, who received his training from the Hermetic Order the Golden Dawn. Prior to the Rider-Waite-Colman-Smith deck, the 56 pip cards (also known as the minor arcana) included within a standard deck did not portray the imagery many of us are accustomed to seeing. However, the modern pictorial design Colman and Waite created has worked spectacularly well, since it provides the reader a scene on which to focus. Depending on the intention of the reader, the cards can be used in a multitude of ways, from divining future events to manifesting secret desires.

One method of reading tarot cards is to intentionally pull out a specific card related to the thing or situation you wish to manifest. Do you wish to manifest a new vehicle for transportation? Well, there is a perfect card for that: The Chariot. Do you wish to have many children? Working with The Empress card would do the trick, as it contains all the appropriate imagery for motherhood and fertility. Assuming that you, the reader, are familiar with the magical arts, you may also want to consider including other powerful correspondences to add extra "oomph" to your spells.

Candles, herbs, precious stones, sigils, and words of intention can be included in tarot readings to create a fabulously effective ritual for manifesting your desires. Be sure to choose your supplies carefully and to have the tarot card in question front and center on your altar to bring in powerful archetypal assistance. As Paul Huson said in *Mastering Witchcraft*, there are "powers existing within the deep minds of all of us, Jungian archetypes, if you like, which can be contracted to bring a certain power to your rituals." Tarot is more than a tool that reveals the future; it can also help you manifest it.

CHAPTER 5

Considerations When Making Magic

As we've established, magic and manifestation can be done rather simply. You don't need a slew of expensive ingredients and a ton of candles lit around you as you stir a huge cauldron. Witchcraft is personal and is different for every individual who practices it. If full-blown rituals aren't your thing, work with days, times, and colors to enhance your craft and strengthen the likelihood of successful manifestation in more subtle ways. In this chapter, you'll learn not only some of the best times to conjure up magic, but also gain insight into the esoteric functions of elements, colors, seasons, numbers, and more. When's the best time to cast a spell? What day should you light the money candle you made? You'll find the answers in this section.

Moon Phases

People have associated the moon with magic since the dawn of time. In ancient Egypt, the moon was associated with Thoth, the god of wisdom and magic. Two of the major goddesses in Greco-Roman religion and mythology, Hecate and Diana, are not only lunar goddesses but also seen as patron goddesses to witches. In tarot, The Moon card represents mystery and the unknown. In Europe, from the medieval times up until the 17th century, it was purported that witches would gather deep in the woods to dance and perform rituals—this was known as a Sabbat. These speculations and practices endured and resurfaced again in the New World.

The moon is said to hold sway over the tides, as well as mental health and the female reproductive system. The light it casts guides us as we navigate through the darkness. There are 13 lunar months, and in witchcraft, these are sometimes observed by covens and called esbats (a word derived from the French word *esbattre*, which means "to frolic"), as a time not necessarily for rituals, but for socializing or performing personal spells. Esbats are generally held monthly or bimonthly, depending on how closely you're working with and around the lunar calendar.

Many witches base their spellwork and manifestations around lunar phases. This makes it easier to coordinate and plan your rituals and spells. Workings for abundance and prosperity would be geared around the waxing moon, while spells to banish or offer protection would be done around the waning moon. Some witches consider the full moon a free-for-all, as this is a time of immense power. The moon plays a predominantly large role in Neo-Pagan faiths such as Wicca, where rituals are often centered around the lunar calendar and primarily the full moon. The moon is seen as an aspect of the Goddess, a central figure in Wicca, which is usually personified as a triple goddess—the Maiden, Mother, and Crone. This personification speaks to the different lunar phases and the different phases of human growth.

Following, we'll explore different lunar phases, their distinct magical attributes and energies, as well as the appropriate spells and rituals for each phase. While working with the moon lends spells a powerful boost, you do not need to sync your entire life with it or strictly schedule around it. On the other hand, if you would like to be more in touch with the cycles, I'd suggest downloading a moon phase app. If you missed the full moon, don't fret; the power of the full moon lasts three days: the full moon day marked on the calendar, the day before, and the day after. After the full moon, it wanes (gets smaller) and then waxes (gets fuller).

New Moon: Representing initiation, new beginnings, and emotional growth, this moon phase is ideal for spells for manifesting travel or a new income, career, or relationship, and new adventures or change.

Waxing Moon: Also called a bright moon or waxing to full, this is the perfect phase for love spells, manifesting. marriage, fertility, luck, and success. It's a potent time to create charms for attraction and sweet jars.

Full Moon: Known as the "witches' Sabbat" (esbat), this phase is useful for purification, spells for renewal, sex magic, divination, psychic enhancement, spirit work, love drawing, cursing and hexing, justice, female empowerment, ancestral veneration, and wish fulfillment.

Waning Moon: A time of endings, the waning moon presents the opportunity to perform spells to heal, release old habits, banish enemies or toxic relationships, and ward off sickness and death.

Dark Moon: Occurring just before the new moon (on the first day of the lunar cycle, the first waxing moon), this sacred night is dedicated to Hecate/Hekate. It's a good time for spirit work, divination, justice spells, reversing fortune, breaking spells, countering magic, astral travel, and bindings.

Other useful lunar associations include deities, crystals and stones, and herbs and plants. Combining them in spellwork with specific lunar phases can increase your manifesting powers.

Lunar deities: Thoth, Hecate/Hekate, Diana, Artemis, Selene, and Khonsu

Lunar crystals/stones: Moonstone, pearl, quartz, selenite, smokey quartz, clear quartz, mother of pearl, black tourmaline, and black kyanite

Lunar herbs/plants: All night-blooming flowers, lotus, sandalwood, chamomile, mushrooms, poppy, St. John's wort, water lily, and pumpkin

Seasons

Seasons are the living proof of magic on earth and play a very important role in our everyday lives, whether we know it or not. Different seasons have different energies that we can tap into as practitioners. Many holidays center around specific seasons and seasonal changes that we will talk about later in this chapter.

Centuries ago, people would huddle together around a fire during the cold months with pelts of fur, telling stories and keeping warm, while manifesting that they'd survive the harsh winter and dreaming about the coming of spring. Today, we still carry on that tradition by communing with family and keeping warm while making hopeful plans for the spring. The magic of the seasons is not something exclusive to just witches. For millennia, we've been doing rituals to promote and honor each season. If you head to your local pharmacy during spring, you're bound to see chocolate bunnies and eggs—imagery that helps manifest renewal and change.

WINTER

This is a time of introspection and rest. Winter is the perfect season for soul-searching and manifesting different aspects of healing, including mental health and clarity. Do you have friends or family members who are toxic or hinder you from achieving your goals? Take advantage of this season and freeze them out. Winter is a time of independence, strength, and letting go. Use the chilling qualities of winter to put up barriers of protection and freeze out negative energy and spirits. Brew a nice, hot cup of loose leaf tea and read in the leaves what the future will hold at the end of winter. There's no better time to manifest better and brighter days.

SPRING

Spring is marked by the ancient Germanic holiday Ostara/Ēostre, also named for the goddess of spring and renewal. This is the time to cleanse and clear out all the bad juju in your life. Cleaning isn't just a mundane task; the psychical act will also clear out unwanted energies that might be lingering. Wash your windows and floors with salt and water, burn some frankincense or dragon's blood, and spiritually fumigate your home and space. Pull back the curtains, open the windows, and let in the light.

Use this time to manifest new beginnings. This is the best time to work spells that promote fertility, love, and passion, as well as abundance and financial growth. Manifest and enhance the attraction of a specific partner by making and sprinkling some Water of Venus (see page 110), or plant a garden with rosemary for protection. Connect with nature by going for walks, visiting a local park, and reading up on your local flora and fauna. Harness the power of spring to banish the old and conjure forth the new. Wear pink and yellow to enhance the power of the season. Incorporate imagery of eggs, bunnies, lambs, and flowers.

FALL

Fall is the time of harvest. Winter is approaching and we must preserve all that we've planted. This is a time of tying up loose ends. Meditate on everything you wish to keep in your life. Spells for protection during this time are well advised.

Fall is also a time of death and endings. Banishing negativity, illness, and malevolence is recommended at this time. Spirit work is also recommended, as the veil between the worlds grows increasingly thin and is thinnest on October 31st, known as Samhain (pronounced Soh-in), or the Witch's New Year.

Using divination is another wonderful way to connect to the energies of fall. As you close one chapter, divination can be used to see what lies ahead. Enhance your divination skills by working with tarot, runes, oracles cards, or any other such tools. Try manifesting connections to spirit guides or call on them for help. Working with spirits or deities of the underworld and moon should also yield results during this time. Don't forget to acknowledge loved ones and ancestors who have passed, as they may be sending messages through the thinned veil.

SUMMER

This is a special time of year that is not only magical for witches, but also for school-age children, families, vacationers, outdoor sports enthusiasts, and pretty much anyone who doesn't have an extreme aversion to the sun. The rain has likely ceased, winter's chill is gone, and both humans and animals can finally emerge from the safety and comfort of their dwellings to discover joy under the warm glow of the sun.

There are many ways witches can connect to the energy of this bright, mirthful season. Probably the most important celebrations recognized by witches and Pagans alike are the first day of summer, also known as midsummer, and the summer solstice, the longest day and shortest night of the year, when the sun's strength is at its zenith. Use the energy of this day to manifest healing, abundance, and love.

Day & Time

◇◇◇◇◇◇◇◇◇◇◇◇

Just as we can work with the magic of the four seasons, we can also plan our manifestations according to the seven days of the week. Furthermore, within each day there are opportune times to work our magic. Different times during the day can be used to either draw something forth or push something away. When the sun rises in the morning is a great time to set your intentions for the day and begin planting the seeds of your desires (or more specifically, the thing or scenario you wish to have come to fruition). When the sun is at its peak, draw down the potent energy of the solar orb to solidify your wish into something more tangible and real. And because the setting sun is all about endings and causing things to disappear, this is a great time to let go of things that no longer serve you.

DAYS

The days of the week present opportunities to tap into different kinds of energies, too, lending your spells and manifestations extra coherence with the natural world.

Monday: This literally means "Moon's Day," which is derived from the Latin *lunae dies*. Monday is an excellent day to honor your favorite lunar god/dess and enhance your relationship to the moon and your spiritual self. Use Monday's energy for workings related to women's health, fertility, motherhood, menstruation, ancestral veneration, female friendships, pregnancy, visions, dreams, psychic development, intuition, divination, peaceful sleep, forgiveness, healing, astral projection, astral travel, higher awareness, purification, clairvoyance, nocturnal animals, prophecies, reconciliation, larceny, protection, household and hearth, and therapy.

Tuesday: Derived from the name of the Norse god Tyr, Tuesday is associated with justice and balance. Tuesday is also associated with the god and planet of Mars. Use this day to relate more to the masculine and for spells and workings for courage, vitality, and strength. This is the perfect time to do magic regarding justice and legal matters as well.

Wednesday: Coming from the Old English meaning "Wodenaz's Day," Wednesday is also known as "Odin's Day" after the Norse god of knowledge and wisdom. Being the day of Mercury as well, it is usually a time to work on magic and spells regarding travel, communication, transportation, art, theater, entertainment, change, luck, gambling, fortune, luxury, wealth, and creativity.

Thursday: Named after the Norse god Thor, Thursday is also the day of Jupiter. Thursday is a great time to perform acts of manifestation associated with leadership, promotion, public figures, authority, achievement, thriving prosperity, boosting notoriety and influence, material gain, grants, dominance, and control over situations.

Friday: Named after the Norse goddess Freya, Friday is the day of Venus, and a time to manifest love and romance. On this day, you can focus on attracting and enhancing relationships, as well as improving self-worth. Fridays are a wonderful time for ritual baths and cleansings.

Saturday: "Saturn's Day," after the planet, is the day for endings, banishings, hexes, uncrossing, breaking bad habits, personal growth, discipline, and setting and breaking down boundaries.

Sunday: "Sun's Day" is dedicated to solar deities and energies. This is a promising time for magic related to development, promotion, enlightenment, studying, knowledge, wisdom, exorcism, general health, riches, growing business, achievement in politics, popularity, prosperity, confidence, and fame.

HOLIDAYS

Within witchcraft and Paganism, there are many ancient holidays that practitioners still celebrate to this day to acknowledge the different facets of the waxing and waning tides of the year. This includes days on which we honor specific spirits and deities. Following are the prominent celebrations that are often used in witchcraft practices, so you may celebrate to promote your manifestation needs. If you are interested in Wicca, you may also wish to follow their wheel of the year, an annual cycle of festivals.

Winter Solstice/Yule (December 21st): The shortest day and the longest night of the year. In Wicca and Celtic Druidry, this day marks the death of the horned god. It is also observed by the Greeks and Romans as the time when Persephone returns to her husband Hades/Pluto in the underworld.

New Year's Day/Kalends of January (January 1st): This day is named after the ancient Roman god Janus. The first of this month is a time of new beginnings. Ring in the new year with spells to promote abundance, happiness, and success.

Walpurgis Night/May Eve (April 30th): Originally celebrated as a day to protect yourself from witchcraft and curses, this holiday has been reclaimed by witches and Pagans as a time when witches would fly off to the sabbat. This holiday is usually celebrated in conjunction with Beltane.

Midsummers Day/Saint John's Eve (June 23rd): This is a time for blessings and renewal. Use this time to cleanse your tools and yourself. A customary tradition in New Orleans Voodoo is to get a "head washing," which is similar to a Voodoo baptism. This leaves the practitioner feeling renewed and regenerated.

Autumn Equinox/Mabon (September 22nd): Sometimes known as the witches' thanksgiving, this is a time of abundance, as we appreciate the gifts of the earth and connect with the fauna, flora, and spirits of nature.

Samhain (October 31st): Pronounced "Soh-in," this is one of the best times for magic and manifestation. Rituals of any kind can be done during this time, although they should be done in tandem with spirit work and divination, as this is the time when the veil between this world and the otherworld is at its thinnest.

TIME

Just like days and holidays, certain hours also have potent energy that can be used in magic and manifestation. We have all had that urge to make a wish when we notice that it is 11:11. Some practitioners refer to these numbers as "angel numbers." I believe these numbers connect us to that liminal space between here and the other realm. For more advanced practitioners, certain times connect with certain planets. Here are a few special times you can choose to help enhance your magical workings.

Dawn: Greet the day with a morning meditation. Cleansings, purification, and healing should be the main focus during this time.

Noon: Use the power of the sun for business and financial success, opportunities, legal matters, and prosperity.

Sunset: This is the best time to perform rituals and spells to assist in breaking addiction or bad habits, as well as releasing things that hold you back.

Midnight: Sometimes known as the witching hour, this is the time to perform your most important spells and rituals. If there are things that you wish to manifest that seem unlikely or require the removal of obstacles, save spellwork for this time.

3 to 4 a.m.: This is the original witching hour, which was widely recognized medieval times all the way up until the 19th century. Use this time for divination and to enhance your psychic awareness. This is also the time for spirit communication, as well as spells to heal old wounds and rituals to relieve stress.

11:11: If you're seeing this number, then it's probably a good time to make a wish. Take the sight of this number as a confirmation that your manifestations will be successful.

Elements

◇◇◇◇◇◇◇◇◇◇◇◇◇

Whether we know it or not, we are connected to the elements; they flow through us and we are imbued with their magic. Our feet connect us to the earth, our breath is enriched with the power of air, our hearts beat with the passion of fire, and our eyes burst with the emotional tides of water.

Witches work with specific elements to enhance manifesting. Each element has its own strengths. In some rituals and altar setups, all the elements are represented, with salt for earth, incense for air, candles for fire, and a bowl of water. While it is customary in most Wiccan and Neo-Pagan practices to honor the spirits and energies of each element during ritual, you may gravitate to one specific element. This could be because of your birth sign and the element associated with it, or simply personal preference. Do you enjoy swimming? Have an affinity for sea creatures? This could be an indication that you are connected to the element of water. Aside from just energies, all elements have spirits associated with them; these are called elementals. They are known throughout the world and have various names. Listed here are the energies and spirits associated with each element.

EARTH

Use the power of earth for spells and rituals regarding prosperity, fertility, growth, money, creativity, and stability. Salt, dirt, clay, and rocks can all be used in amulets and charms for maintaining balance and staying grounded. Call on the forces of earth when you feel weak, unbalanced, emotionally unstable, or need to find a place to live. Earth's energy will help you manifest new career opportunities or long-term goals.

Lay on the ground, walk barefoot, go for a walk or hike in nature, or sit underneath a tree and read or brainstorm something you wish to manifest. Crystals associated with the earth are agate, bloodstone, emerald, tigers eye, and smoky quartz. Earth corresponds to the zodiac sign Taurus and the planet Venus. Colors associated with earth are green, brown, and black. Herbs/plants associated with the earth include all root vegetables, wheat, oak, ivy, licorice, corn, and rye. Animals such as bulls, bison, stags, and snakes all bear earth's energy. Gnomes, dryads, nymphs, and fairies are spirits of the earth. Earth goddesses include Cybele/Magna Mater (Roman), Danu (Celtic), Demeter (Greek), Fauna (Roman), Mother Goddess (Wiccan), Gaia (Greek), and Pomona (Roman). Earth gods include Attis (Roman), Baal (Syrian-Hebrew), Bacchus (Roman), Dionysus (Greek), and Osiris (Egyptian).

AIR

The element of air is perfect for assisting with workings that need to be done rather quickly or require travel. It was said during colonial times that witches could fly through the air. They were also known to bring about great gusts of wind or call down storms.

Send your manifestations and spells through the air with a little help from the wind. The planet Mercury is associated with air, which enhances our connection to communication and travel. The zodiac signs associated with air are Gemini, Libra, and Aquarius. Tap into air energy by wearing white or pale yellow.

You may wish to meditate on imagery of balloons, bubbles, sounds, and windmills, or incorporate the symbolism into your spellwork. Plants and herbs associated with air include vervain, primrose, fern, yarrow, and aspen. Animals associated with air include birds, flying insects, and bats. Call on air to enhance your psychic work and send telepathic messages to spirits. Air elementals include sylphs and sprites. Deities associated with air include Mercury (Roman), Hermes (Greek), Gabriel (Catholic), and Zephyrus (Greco-Roman).

FIRE

Want to send something out into the universe? Burn it. In ancient Greece, Egypt, and Rome, priests and practitioners would burn up offerings to appease the gods. It was said that the smoke from the burnt offerings would rise up and reach the heavens.

Fire is associated with creation. Harness the energy of fire to enhance spells and rituals regarding sex, passion, purification, and courage. Candle magic is one of the most prominent ways to use the element of fire. Bonfires and fireplaces can also be used to burn wishes, petitions, and offerings.

The heavenly bodies associated with fire are the sun, Mars, and Jupiter. Crystals associated with fire include citrine, fire opal, and garnet. Its astrological signs are Aries, Leo, and Sagittarius. Colors associated with fire include gold, crimson, red, and orange. Burn copal, frankincense, or myrrh. Call on fire to ignite passion, motivation, and inspiration, and assist with leadership, authority, and the power over others. The djinn and salamanders are potent fire spirits. Deities include Astarte (Mesopotamian), Bridget (Celtic), Hestia (Greek), Ogün (Yoruba and Vodoun), Sekhmet (Egyptia), Vesta (Roman), and Vulcan (Roman).

WATER

Water is a conduit to the other realm; it is also where we see a reflection of ourselves. It cleans us and revitalizes us, offering us renewal. Water is beneficial for spells and rituals that assist in healing, purification, cleansing, and psychic work. Its energy is feminine and ethereal.

The heavenly bodies associated with water are Neptune, Venus, Saturn, and the moon. Crystals associated with water are clear quartz, coral, jade, pearl, and mother of pearl. In witchcraft, the tools of the chalice and cauldron are associated with water. Cancer, Scorpio, and Pisces are its associated zodiac signs. Its colors include blue, aqua, turquoise, and green. Plants include water lily, lotus, moss, reeds, seaweed, and fungi. Animals associated with water include dolphins, crocodiles, alligators, water-dwelling snakes, and generally all marine life. Spirits include merfolk, sirens, kelpie, and undines. Goddesses include Amphitrite (Greek), Aphrodite (Greek), Erzuli (Voudon), Nimue (Celtic), Oshun (Yoruba), and Yemaya (Santeria). Gods of water are Agwe (Voudon), Dylan (Celtic), Neptune (Roman), and Poseidon (Greek).

Colors

◇◇◇◇◇◇◇◇◇◇◇◇

It is a proven fact that color stimulates the senses. Likewise, colors can also stimulate vibrational energies and enhance manifestation. Colors are recognized for their potential in magic and are given special properties in witchcraft and spellwork.

We are influenced by the magic of color all the time. Red gives off vibrations that trigger cravings and indulgence, and is therefore used in decor for restaurants. Blue and white represent tranquility, and are often used in the decor of spas, doctors' offices, and hotels.

Incorporating colors and their energies in your manifestation techniques can be as simple as wearing a T-shirt with the color you wish to use. Match the associated color with what it is you wish to manifest, and you will see your magic enhance tenfold. Following is a list of colors and their associations, as well as some facts about their use in magic and manifestation. Colors also align with your personal vibrations and how you feel when you use them. Don't be afraid to mix and match colors. You can add the energy of the colors through the use of candles, altar cloths, crystals, or matching other magical tools to a color.

RED

Life force, attraction, sensuality, desire, virility, and strength are associated with red. Red is also the color of death, fire, violence, love, and sex. It is the color of our life force. It's the sacred color of the goddesses Isis and Lilith as well. Use red in spells and rituals regarding vitality, strength, and health. This prominent color is also useful in gaining luck and courage, and for situations when you need a little more attention and focus on yourself. While a popular choice for love spells, keep in mind that the color red exudes a very sexual energy. If you are seeking long-term romance, monogamy, or marriage, make sure that the intention is clear. Use red in spellwork for achieving goals, overcoming obstacles, or performing sex magic.

Red corresponds to Aries and is linked with Mars. In ancient Greece, red was considered a color of life and was used in rituals of necromancy to speak to spirits. Red apples, pomegranates, toadstools, and berries are all considered foods of the gods, so you can always implement these in spellwork to entice deities and spirits to assist in your workings.

ORANGE

Orange promotes positive energy, exuberance, and courage, and is linked to solar energy and magic. Useful in spellwork for obtaining positive outcomes, job success, and wish fulfillment, use orange if you are being considered for a new job. Orange is associated with the planet Mercury and the element of fire. Because orange represents the turning of the leaves in fall as well, it can be used in spells dealing with change, transformation, and alchemy.

YELLOW

Yellow exudes brilliance, joy, and clarity. Use yellow to promote clairvoyance and insight, or when seeking the truth in spellwork. Yellow is a popular candle color for unhexing, uncrossing, and protection spells. It is also linked to solar deities such as Apollo, Horus, and Mithras. Use yellow candles when seeking healing guidance, or to brighten your mood and expel depression. Overall, yellow can be used for rituals that invoke happiness and encourage healing from an operation or illness.

GREEN

Green is now most commonly associated with money, abundance, and greed. However, to the ancient Egyptians, it was the color of life, fertility, and youth. Green is also a fairy color in Celtic folklore, connecting us to the other world. Earth and Venus are the fixed planets for the color green, and water and earth are its associated elements. Green is also associated with Taurus. Green exudes strong vibrations of luck, prosperity, and wealth. Green energy is also potent for those wishing to bear children, and in turn can be used for fertility and sex magic. It is the sacred color of Osiris, Cernunnos, Pan, Ogün, and Demeter.

BLUE

Blue is an ethereal color that connects to the heavenly and divine. Blue is sacred to Zeus, Yemaya, Mary, and Nut, the Egyptian goddess of the sky and heavens. Its associated element is water, and Saturn and Jupiter are its corresponding planets. Blue can be used to promote strength in healing spells. Blue also neutralizes intense vibrations—and can be used to induce a sense of peace and tranquility—which makes it a popular candle color for house cleansings and energy work. Blue novena, or "pull out," candles can be used to petition saints and deities for specific workings.

PINK

The color pink is the essence of "true love." Sacred to the gods Aphrodite, Venus, and Erzuli, pink is the color of emotional love. It represents affection, compassion, beauty, and fidelity. Pink can be used in spellwork to promote romantic relationships, monogamy, and marriage. It is best used in rituals to attract new love and happiness. The color pink can be useful to temper and heal feuds between friends, dispel anger, and promote a sense of harmony amongst relationships.

PURPLE

Purple, the color of royalty and the divine, connects us to power and the supernatural. When you come across purple flowers, consider it a blessing from the deities above. Purple is sacred to Maman Brigitte, Dionysus, Bacchus, and Ghede. Purple can be used in spellwork that requires a lot of energy, when you feel that the desired goal may be difficult to achieve, or to gain personal/financial independence. Purple is a high vibrational color and therefore well suited for spirit work, trance meditation, and astral travel. Burn purple candles for psychic insight and when performing divination, or keep an amethyst with your tarot cards or divination tools.

BROWN

Brown represents the earth—both the element and the planet itself. Because of its strong vibrations of strength and balance, you can use the color brown to draw upon stability. It works well in spells for justice, earth magic, animal/pet spells, and attracting nature spirits. You can

also use the color brown in rituals for grounding, levelhead-
edness, or when you need strength and courage to make a
difficult decision or choice.

BLACK

Despite the misguided negative connotations that caused
the color black to be considered evil, the color black historically represented life. The ancient Egyptians referred to
their land as "Kemet," literally meaning "black land," in
reference to the rich soil of the Nile plains.

It is important to note that the color black and its
association with evil and baneful magic comes from bias
and cultural racism. Magic using the color black is often
perceived as evil, low, dirty, and primitive, while that which
is white is perceived as good, pure, and clean. In reality,
black contains all colors, and is the absence of light, making
it a wonderful tool for absorbing and deflecting negative
energy, spirits, curses and hexes.

A color of wisdom and death, black symbolizes resur-
rection and renewal. Black is associated with the planet
Saturn and the elements earth and water. It is the color of
the dark and waning moon and is sacred to Hecate, Nyx,
and Diana. Black candles can be used in spells for binding,
banishing, uncrossing, and exorcism.

WHITE

The absence of color makes white one of the strongest
"colors" for spellwork. White is connected to the spiritual
realm, innocence, wonder, purity, and new beginnings. It's
connected to the moon and all the elements—earth, wind,
fire, air, and spirit. White is sacred to Hathor, Ceridwen/
Cerridwen, Isis, Chango, and the Triple Goddess.

White candles can be used in spells for clarity, protection, meditation, and angel magic. The color of milk, white is often linked to life, fertility, and nourishment. In many folk magic practices, it is known as a highly symbolic color of goodness and balance. White is also the color of bone, linking it with death and structure. The color of snow, it can be used to freeze other energies or disturbances and protect from outside forces. In general, you can think of the color white as a blank canvas ready to be transformed; it is the beginning and the end. Use a white altar cloth to attract inspiration and creativity, or to create a sacred space.

The Zodiac

Astrology involves divining the future through the charting of planetary constellations. While astrology itself dates back to ancient Mesopotamia around the second millennium BCE, today's astrology has its roots in ancient Rome, around the fourth century CE. Astrologers in ancient Rome would chart the planets and keep an eye out for omens that would predict the outcome of a current war, the political climate, or even the next ruler. Astrology was also used as a way to chart the appropriate time to perform surgery or attempts to heal. During the Renaissance, famed occultists synchronized the practices of magic and astrology, and they've worked hand in hand ever since.

When it comes to manifestations, you may wish to follow the wisdom of the ancient Romans and plan your spells around certain astrological signs. If you want to generate additional cash flow or wish to purchase a home, performing an abundance spell during Taurus season would be wise. Don't want to wait till May to perform that spell? You can perform the spell when the moon is in Taurus. The moon takes an average of about 28 days to orbit the earth, during which time it passes through all 12 zodiac houses. This means that the moon passes through a different sign roughly every two days. Let's now dive into the zodiac signs and some of the best ways to use them in conjunction with your manifestation and magic.

ARIES

The time coinciding with the sign of Aries is a time of high vibrations. Spells and rituals to assist in new projects and travel are advisable. This sign is filled with a warrior-like energy, and therefore can assist you in overcoming obstacles and obtaining positions of authority and power. The full moon in Aries is a wonderful time for meditating and manifesting change in your routine. If you feel overwhelmed or insecure, carry a bloodstone with you or wear some iron jewelry during this time to enhance the energy. You might also wish to incorporate colors such as red and burgundy to enhance the sign's energy.

TAURUS

Taurus is an earth sign and is ruled by the planet Venus, as well as the moon. Use the moon in Taurus for manifestation and magic of all kinds. Perform spells to attract attention during this time, whether that's gaining fame or getting your boss to notice your good work. Taurus energy provides stability, fertility, and luxury. In addition to being useful for generating material gains, Taurus energy can be used to enhance relationships and find committed partners through the use of love magic. Wear green to promote

Taurus energy, and carry a piece of tumbled turquoise to ground yourself and attract stable income.

GEMINI

Representing the divine twins, Gemini is the third sign of the zodiac and is associated with happiness, luck, and success. The Gemini full moon is a perfect time to make wishes and focus on manifesting creative endeavors. Spellwork to encourage success in school or starting a new business it is also advisable during this time. Authors might want to send in their manuscripts around this time. Need a vacation? Manifest one during the new moon in Gemini. Agate, citrine, peridot, and tigers eye are all useful crystals to enhance what you wish to accomplish during the Gemini moon.

CANCER

The time for serenity, sensitivity, and tranquility, Cancer's energy is useful for meditation and to gain peace of mind. The full moon and Cancer are dedicated to spells regarding health, family, and comfort. Gift a small piece of tumbled moonstone to friends or family that may need support and comfort. Since Cancer energy is about comfort, you may wish to manifest things such as protection for your home, or to attract household spirits. Are you lonely? Manifest a furry companion or relationship. Ritual cleansings and rituals of purification should be performed during the new moon in Cancer.

LEO

This energy exudes ego and a demand for attention. Use this energy to persuade those who may wish to say no to you. Sweet jars, poppets, and candle magic regarding intimacy, employment, promotion, and entertainment are all especially potent during this time. Carry a small piece of amber or topaz to enhance the Leo energy. Create an altar or give offerings to solar deities to obtain their favor during this time. The full moon in Leo can also assist in workings related to fertility and childbirth. Manifestations that require people's attention on you should be performed during this time.

VIRGO

Virgo is a sign dedicated to details and focus. This is the time to manifest organization and structure. If you feel that things have been chaotic or off balance, harness the Virgo energy to assist you in enhancing your organizational skills. Use the energy of the full moon in Virgo to overcome laziness and lethargy as well. Place some rosemary and lavender in a small, green felt bag and keep it with you to assist with remaining grounded and avoiding distraction. The full moon in Virgo is another wonderful time to manifest employment, job security, and financial stability. Work spells to enhance social networking and business partnerships.

LIBRA

Use this sign's energy to enhance your intellect and manifest help in regard to justice, legal matters, and balance. The full moon in Libra is also a good time for love spells and rituals for healing, especially those related to broken bones. Would you like to convince someone to see things your way? This is a time to do it. Bust out a sweet jar and put your persuasion skills to work. Use the energy of Libra to bring about balance in romantic relationships and friendships. Carrying a clear quartz crystal with you will enhance the magical properties of Libra.

SCORPIO

When the moon enters this sign, be prepared for intense emotions, both passionate and chaotic. This is an appropriate time to release bad habits. Since emotions may be high during this time, you may wish to carry a piece of hematite with you to avoid taking everything personally and to deflect negative energy. Incorporate the color black into your wardrobe to enhance protection and banish unwanted negativity. The full moon in Scorpio is a perfect time to work on strengthening your psychic abilities. Focus on manifesting self-love and positive transformation. Considering the intense energy of the sign, it is also a time to amplify your knowledge of witchcraft and perhaps work on building relationships with spirits and deities.

SAGITTARIUS

The vibrations and energies this moon gives off is often impulsive and adventurous, and may lead you outside of your comfort zone. Use this time to manifest feelings of optimism and work spells for travel and leisure. Want to explore the country? Meditate on it during this time. This is also a time to work spells aimed at success. Would you like to attract more clients to your business? Carry the Temperance card from a tarot deck in your wallet. Looking to make a business proposal? Wear a splash of red. Don't focus too much on matters that might bring you down.

CAPRICORN

Looking to get things moving in your career? The Capricorn moon is here to instill you with all the vibrational force you need to get to work. Manifestations regarding overcoming difficult situations, completing drawn-out projects, and achieving career aspirations are all within the realm of this sign. Focus on spells to bring about independence and discipline, and assist you in making decisions. The full moon in Capricorn is perfect for meditation and relaxation as well, since Capricorn energy is soothing. This is also a good time to work on magic for healing and assistance with diet and nutrition.

AQUARIUS

The vibes of this sign are nomadic, spiritual, and wise. Manifest deeper connections with people during this time, and focus on ways to enhance creativity and build a deeper connection to the spirit realm. Spellwork and rituals should be done during this moon phase to promote social justice and bring about equality. Workings, rituals, and group spells will be extremely potent under an Aquarius moon. Remove The Star card from your tarot deck and carry it with you during a full moon in Aquarius to assist you in making manifestation come to fruition, or carry a piece of onyx with you.

PISCES

The moon in Pisces is a great time for creative endeavors. The vibrations of this moon are fantastical, ethereal, and enchanting. Would you like to get away from working a 9-to-5 job while still having the financial stability to pursue your art? Wrap moonstone and some poppyseeds in green cloth to carry in your left pocket underneath the Pisces moon to manifest that. Hone your astral projection skills or delve into past lives during this time. When the moon is full in Pisces, try painting, drawing, or writing—anything to get those creative juices flowing.

Numbers

Numbers are very useful in magic and spellwork. As a matter of fact, the use of numbers is prominent in many spells and rituals. You may need to recite an incantation a certain number of times, use a certain number of ingredients in spells, or tie a certain number of knots when doing knot magic. The association of numbers with magic goes back to ancient Egypt and can be seen throughout history, specifically in medieval texts and written accounts during the witch trials of the 16th and 17th century in Europe and North America. Many charms and spells in folk magic use the magic of numbers. Following are a few of the most popular numbers used in magic and witchcraft. You can use these numbers as a guide to add or take out ingredients, repeat invocations, or tie knots.

One is actually not the loneliest number; rather, it is a symbol of achievement, new beginnings, leadership, and the spark of creation. Use this number in spells to increase originality and stand out from the rest.

Two is the number of love, passion, justice, commitment, and duality.

Three represents the sacred trinity. Dedicated to the Triple Goddess and trinity deities such as Hecate, it represents beginnings, middles, and endings; the three phases of life; and the three phases of the moon; as well as mind, body, and spirit. Tie three knots to seal charm bags.

Four is a powerful number to assist in manifesting completeness and stability. This number was considered sacred in ancient Egypt and correlates with the four elements of nature, as well as the four cardinal points and directions.

Five is the number of protection, as in the pentacle, which has five points. The number five is also useful in spells and workings for attraction, love, spiritual awakening, and conjuring spirits.

Six is associated with the sun and solar deities. It also corresponds to the planets Mercury and Venus. Incorporate the number six in spells to attract love, fertility, and material wealth.

Seven is the spiritual number associated with Jehovah. It was also said to be a favorite of Pythagoras. Use seven in spells to gain knowledge, reveal truth, gain clarity, or raise spiritual vibrations.

Eight is the number of infinity, success, renewal, and Mercury.

Nine, the number of the moon, is useful in lunar rituals, and is sacred to the nine muses, as well as all moon deities. Tie nine knots when doing bindings or rituals for protection and dominance.

Ten is the number of completeness. Incorporate the number 10 when working manifestations that require something to be completed or finished, such as a project or court case.

Eleven is a number of intuition and self-reflection.

Twelve is another number of completion. Just as there are 12 houses in the zodiac, the number 12 represents power, cosmic forces, and planetary magic.

Thirteen is the number of the witch. In traditional witchcraft, there are typically 13 witches in a coven. There are also 13 lunar months, so the number 13 is connected to the moon. Use the number 13 in spells and rituals to boost their potency and power.

CHAPTER 6

Practical Spells & Rituals for Manifestation

Do you think you're ready to cast a spell and conjure up some magic? We have covered the basics and discussed the techniques needed for manifestation and magic, but now it's time to apply those practices. Compiled in this chapter are spells and rituals that can assist you on your sacred journey. The majority of these spells come from folk magic and are therefore simple, requiring minimal and easy-to-find tools and ingredients. Ingredients, as well as possible customizations, are listed to suit your individual needs. Remember that at the end of the day, the power comes from you. If you are missing an ingredient or are not within a certain moon phase that is suggested for the spell, do what feels right and use substitutions as needed.

What You Need

You really don't need much to manifest what you desire; however, witchcraft tends to harness its magic from nature and the use of tools. Here are a few beneficial tools and ingredients to have on hand for your workings, spells, and rituals. I've broken down the tools and ingredients you'll need into "must-haves," which you absolutely need to carry out the spells in this book, and "nice-to-haves," which may be suggested but could be substituted.

Must-Haves:

- Candles of various sizes and colors are good to have on hand; however, chime candles are preferred, as they burn through quickly and are cost effective. The most common candle colors to have on hand are black, white, green, pink, and red.
- Salt is perfect for cleansing and protection, so make sure there's always some nearby.
- Herbs are great allies for manifestations, and while you don't need to buy every herb and spice at the grocery store, some to have on hand include vervain, lavender, bay leaves, thyme, mugwort, cinnamon, rose, and rosemary, the most versatile and magical.
- Matches to light your spell candles aflame, and for setting things such as petition papers on fire, should be kept on hand. Matches also contain sulfur, which is perfect for banishing negative vibes. (Remember, fire safety first, always!)
- An incense burner, such as a shell or ceramic dish, will do just fine; just be sure to line the bottom with salt or sand to provide extra insulation and

protect your tabletop from the heat radiating from the bottom of the dish. A coaster underneath the incense burner offers protection for your ritual space as well.

- Incense, both sticks and resins, are good to have on hand. Frankincense, myrrh, and dragon's blood all have lovely aromas and are used to cleanse and bless your space, as well as ward off thwarting energies.
- Cords of various colors and sizes are useful for knot magic.
- A mortar and pestle is needed to crush and bruise herbs.
- Feathers of various sizes can be used to fan incense and make amulets, charms, and spellwork.
- Crystals such as quartz, hematite, amethyst, and citrine will always serve you well.
- Water can be an offering, used in cleansing, and for purification spellwork.
- Mason jars of your preferred size are used for sweetening spells and for combining and storing ingredients.
- Olive oil, which was originally used as a ritual and anointing oil by the ancient Greeks, has many magical properties, making it a preferred oil for anointing tools and making herbal infusions.
- Red and black pens will be useful for writing down petitions and intentions, and journaling about your experiences.
- A notebook not only lets you write down your thoughts, but also provides paper for spellwork requiring petitions and intentions to be written down.
- Scrap cloth, felt bags, or organza bags are used to make charm bags.

Nice-to-Haves:

- Candles: Figure candles and novena/seven-day candles
- Crystals: Lapiz lazuli, malachite, onyx, black tourmaline, moonstone, lodestone, tigers eye, amber, and carnelian
- Herbs: High John root, cinquefoil (five-finger grass), hyssop, wormwood, oak, cedar, dandelion, rue, St. John's wort, devil's claw, and damiana
- Oils: Rose, jasmine, patchouli, eucalyptus, and Egyptian musk
- Cauldron: To make and burn incense, as well as mix up magical concoctions
- Altar cloth: To decorate your altar and make a space of spiritual focus, as well as to protect your table from ash, wax, and herb spills
- Chalice: To represent the element of water and hold offering beverages, such as wine, ale, and juice
- Besom (broom): To sweep away negative energies, clear sacred space, and place by the door, bristles up, for protection
- Candle holders: To prevent candles from tipping over, and for aesthetic
- Deity figures: To represent specific deities you'd like to call in
- Tarot cards: For personal guidance and connecting with guides
- Pendulum: To connect with spirits, guides, and your higher self by asking yes/no questions
- *Farmers' Almanac*: To chart planets
- Dagger or knife: To use as a ritual blade and direct energy

Customizable Spells & Rituals

Witches are resourceful because they see the magic in everything. Belief in animism, or the idea that spirits reside in everything from nature, ensures that the majority of tools and ingredients that witches use enhance the vibrations of spellwork and help with manifestation. Following are a few folk spells and charms that are rather simple and require ingredients that are easily accessible. Many of the spells can be used for multiple purposes with just a simple change of a color, crystal, or herb. Customizing spells and rituals will become easier the more you become familiar with the meanings of different correspondences. Additionally, many of the spells call for many of the same tools and ingredients from the must-haves section of this book (see pages 102 and 103). This is because one crystal or herb can contain many vibrations that can be harnessed to assist in a variety of different manifestations and magic.

SPELL POUCH

A common tool to have on hand, a spell pouch is not only simple to make but also extremely versatile and can be used to assist in almost every scenario. Change the contents of the pouch and its color, and you will have a completely different charm bag for a completely different situation. Get a small drawstring pouch. (These can be purchased on Amazon, at craft stores, or at any metaphysical store.) Fill the pouch with three pinches of the specific herb or herbs that correspond to what it is you wish to manifest. Then place a crystal with the same correspondence in the pouch. Tie the pouch closed with three knots.

- **LOVE:** herbs—damiana or rose petals; crystal—rose quartz

- **PROTECTION:** herbs—rosemary or vervain; crystals—onyx or hematite

- **HEALING:** herbs—lavender, oak, or rosemary; crystals—carnelian or quartz

ENCHANTMENT SPRAY

Think of enchantment spray like a potion bottle—one spritz, and manifestation is put into action. The recipe for the spray is not only super simple, but extremely versatile as well. It's also discreet, so you may work your enchantment almost anywhere. Fill a spray bottle halfway with vodka, add a few pinches of the corresponding herb, a small tumbled stone/crystal, and three drops of the appropriate essential oil. Top the rest of the bottle off with water and secure the cap. Shake well. If the spell is intended to attract someone to you, lightly mist yourself prior to seeing them or the area where they will be. Personal spaces can also be misted to change the vibrations of the space.

- **LOVE:** herbs—rose petals or damiana; oils—jasmine or rose; crystal—rose quartz

- **CLEANSE/CLEAR:** herb—rosemary; oils—patchouli or frankincense; crystals—hematite or clear quartz

- **PROSPERITY:** herbs—bay or rosemary; oils—lemon, cinnamon, or mint; crystal—citrine

MAGICAL BURN BUNDLES

Almost every civilization throughout history has burned herbs for ritualistic purposes. While the first thing that may come to mind is the burning of white sage, this is actually taken from a ceremonial act known as "smudging" and is specific to Native American culture. However, there are many other herbs and plants that can be burned aside from sage in what I like to call "spiritual fumigation." Take the branches or leaves from the plant and bunch them together, then wrap the bundle with a thin piece of cord or thread. Secure with a knot. Burn the end and use your hand or a feather to fan the smoke. Remember to leave a window or door open to have a place for the energies to exit.

- ◆ **CLEANSE/PROTECT:** rosemary or cedar

- ◆ **BYE-BYE BAD VIBES:** rosemary, rue, or lavender

- ◆ **SPIRIT ATTRACTION:** mugwort, also known as black sage

WITCH'S LADDER

A popular charm amongst witches, this simple spell can be made for a variety of purposes. As with the previous spells, you need only alter the color to change the purpose. The magic of this spell comes from the energy directed at the knots. To begin, take three cords of the same length, one red, one black, and the third in the color associated with what you wish to manifest. Focusing on your intent, braid the cords together, making knots every so often after a braided section to secure your intent. Traditionally a witch's ladder is composed of nine knots; however, you may tie as many as you wish (see pages 96 through 98 about number correspondences to find one that suits your needs). Feathers of different colors can also be tied to enhance the ladder's vibration. When complete, pass it through incense, give it a kiss, and hide it in a secret place.

WITCH'S BOTTLE

Originally used as a form of counter-magic to deter witches and protect against witchcraft, this 17th-century charm has been reclaimed by witches and is used primarily for protection against spirits and malefic forces. However, you can also use it to protect against outside influences that could affect your manifestations and magic. Get a small glass bottle, and place three nails, three pins, and three sewing needles inside. Fill the bottle with salt, seal the bottle, and bury it in your back yard or leave it in a dark corner of your home, such as the back of your closet. If you wish to protect your home or someone else's, you may also add dirt from the property to the bottle.

Spells & Rituals for Common Issues & Goals

The following spells and rituals have been gathered from various tomes, grimoires, and historical texts, the majority of which have been altered and tweaked for modern-day use, as well as made to be more practical for the modern witch on the go. No more digging up root of yew in a graveyard during a full moon, although that sounds super fun.

ELEMENTAL POWER CHARM

To perform manifestations, we must be balanced and properly connected to earth, as well as to the divine. This powerful charm incorporates items that contain powerful attributes of all the elements. Keep this charm with you when you wish to remain focused and increase your manifestations skills.

- ◆ Seashell (water)
- ◆ Small, green drawstring bag
- ◆ Pinch salt (earth)
- ◆ Small feather (air)
- ◆ Match (fire)

1 Hold the seashell in both your hands, close your eyes, and visualize waves crashing against a beach. Place the seashell in the bag.

2 Sprinkle a pinch of salt in the bag while being aware of the ground beneath you. This is the power of the earth supporting you.

3 Wave the feather in front of you, fanning the air. Imagine a gust of wind blowing around you. Place the feather in the bag.

4 Hold the unlit match it in your hand, making a fist. Feel the heat radiating from the match. After a few moments of clutching the match, place it in the bag.

5 Secure the charm bag with three knots and keep it on your altar, or bring it out whenever you wish to engage in manifestation spellwork.

WATER OF VENUS

This enchantment spray comes from an 18th-century love potion commonly referred to as "angel's water." Throughout most of Europe and the British Isles, it was traditionally made with an herb called myrtle, associated with the goddess of love, Aphrodite/Venus; however, this specific recipe is from a Spanish formula. Spray it to enhance feelings of passion and to attract both physical and romantic relationships. You may also spray it on yourself to enhance self-love, or mist bedsheets, clothing, or even something belonging to the person you wish to attract.

- ◆ Glass spray bottle
- ◆ Water
- ◆ Vodka
- ◆ 3 drops lavender essential oil
- ◆ 3 drops rose essential oil
- ◆ Pinch dried angelica

1 Fill the bottle halfway with water and the rest of the way with vodka.

2 Add three drops each of lavender essential oil and rose essential oil to the bottle, focusing on the different aspects of love you wish to attract.

3 Add a pinch of angelica to the bottle and secure the cap.

4 Hold the bottle between your hands and say, "Beautiful Venus, goddess divine, let this enchantment bring a love that is mine."

5 Shake the bottle, focusing your energy and desires into the glass.

6 Spray as needed.

VERVAIN MANIFESTATION MAGNET

Vervain is an herb that is common in European folk magic and witchcraft. This simple charm is perfect for carrying with you when you need a little energy boost, or wish to enhance your spellwork and manifestation abilities. Clear quartz is a potent stone for directing energy and enhancing the magical properties of other tools. Carry this charm in your pocket or keep it by your nightstand or desk to promote focus, inspiration, and creativity.

- 1 (2-by-3-inch) white piece of cloth
- 3 pinches vervain
- 1 piece tumbled or raw clear quartz
- Cord, long enough to tie 3 knots

1 Lay out the piece of cloth and sprinkle the vervain in the center the fabric. Lay your hands over the herb and say, "Enchanted herb from days of yore, enhance my power forevermore."

2 Place the quartz in the center of the cloth, on top of the herbs. Lay your hands over the crystal and say, "Crystal quartz, enhance this spell, and make my manifestations go well."

3 Pull up all the corners of the cloths and twist them together; this will create a little bag. Secure the twisted cloth with the cord and tie it with 3 knots.

4 Hold the completed magnet in your hands. Close your eyes and visualize the charm radiating with a blue aura. Sleep with it under your pillow for one night, and then keep it on your altar until it's required for further use.

LOVE SPELL NUMBER 9

This spell is beneficial to those who wish to manifest a monogamous relationship with someone they are currently dating or romantically interested in. Perform the spell during a full moon or on a Friday evening to take advantage of the Venus energy.

- 1 drop rose essential oil
- Red candle (size and shape is up to you, although a figure candle, seven-day candle, or chime candle is preferred)
- Heatproof dish or plate (preferably ceramic)
- Pinch dried jasmine
- Pinch chili powder
- Pinch lavender
- Red cord, long enough to tie 9 knots
- Small red cotton drawstring bag (optional)

1 Place a drop of rose essential oil on top of the red candle, then rub the oil into the candle, working your way from the top, near the wick, toward the bottom of the candle. When you're done, place the candle standing up on the dish.

2 Sprinkle a pinch of jasmine over the candle as you say (either out loud or silently), "Sacred herb and ancient flower, enchant my lover, let them feel your power."

3 Sprinkle a pinch of chili powder over the candle and say, "Ignite with passion, ignite with fire, my love will crave for my desire."

4 Sprinkle a pinch of lavender over the candle and say, "I have the fire, I have the lust, now make this love one I can trust."

5 Take the red cord and speak the desired person's name (out loud or in your mind) as you tie each knot, and continue this process until you have tied 9 knots.

6 Arrange the knotted cord around the candle.

7 Light the candle and let it burn for at least an hour. (If you have chosen a chime candle, let it burn down completely in one sitting.)

8 When the candle has finished burning, hide the knotted cord under your mattress.

9 If there are any wax remnants or herbs left over, you may collect those and put them in a small, red cotton bag to make an additional love charm, or bury it in your backyard.

SELF-LOVE SORCERY

Many people who are attracted to the idea of spells and magic go straight to workings of love in hopes of gaining a partner. But how can you love others if you don't love yourself? This ritual is intended to instill self-love for and confidence in yourself. It requires nothing but a mirror (preferably full-length), maybe some mood lighting, and a sprinkle of honesty and faith. Perform the spell on a Friday evening, or whenever you feel love vibrations or insecurity. Give yourself adequate time to be alone, so that you won't be disturbed.

- ◆ Matches or lighter
- ◆ Candles
- ◆ Music
- ◆ Full-length mirror

1 Set the mood, light a few candles, and play some meditation music.

2 Stand in front of the mirror, stare at yourself, concentrating on your features, then let your eyes wander, glancing at every inch of yourself. Close your eyes and visualize the best version of yourself—mentally, physically, and emotionally.

3 Staring in the mirror and looking at your eyes, say, "Mirror, mirror in front of me, reflect the me I wish to be."

4 Continue to stare at the mirror, and feel yourself merging with your reflection. Think of all the good parts about yourself. What do you love about yourself? Don't be afraid to be vulnerable.

5 Looking at yourself in the mirror, say, "I love you in the looking glass, I love you in the magic mirror, I love you staring back at me, I love the person standing before me."

6 Continue staring at yourself until you believe the words you just spoke.

7 Repeat this ritual consecutively on a Friday evening for the rest of the month to enhance the manifestation and secure the feelings of self-love.

OH, FOR PUCK'S SAKE

Do you feel out of sorts? Perhaps things haven't been going your way lately, or things are happening that cause you to feel irritable? Pesky spirits or fairies might be running amok just to have a laugh, even if it's at your expense. Use a bit of Shakespearean flair to straighten out Puck, the malicious fairy from medieval English folklore, and all the other tricksters that may be messing with your vibes. Perform this quick and simple spell on a Wednesday evening during an even hour.

- Matches or lighter
- Green chime candle
- Silver coin (e.g., a quarter)

1 Use a match or lighter to melt the bottom of the candle, then place it on the silver coin. Make sure the wax hardens so the candle can safely stand in place.

2 Place both hands over the candle and say, "Oh blessed Puck, return my luck."

3 Light the candle and let it burn down completely. Imagine all the stress leaving your body, things going back to normal, and your irritability burning away.

4 When the candle has completely burned out, pick up the coin and hold it between your hands and say, "If we shadows have offended, think but this, and all is mended."

5 Hide the coin in the back of a drawer to appease the spirits, and watch your luck turn around.

"CHA-CHING" MONEY SPRAY

This recipe comes directly from my personal book of spells. You can use it to spray yourself, personal checks, your credit/debit card, bills, coins, and even resumes and business cards to enhance prosperity and incur financial gain.

- Glass spray bottle
- Water
- Vodka
- 3 whole cloves
- 3 drops cinnamon essential oil
- 2 drops lemon balm essential oil
- 2 drops patchouli essential oil

1 Fill the bottle halfway with water, and the rest of the way with vodka.

2 Drop 3 cloves into the bottle and say, "By the power of three, grant me prosperity."

3 Add the drops of cinnamon, lemon balm, and patchouli essential oil, screw the cap on, and shake well.

4 Hold the bottle in your hands and say, "Prosperity, please come this way, abundance resides within this spray."

5 Mist whenever you need some cash flow or to enhance wealth.

LADY OF THE LAKE LEADERSHIP SPELL

We've all heard tales of King Arthur, but remember that he did not achieve that success on his own. He had help from a wise sorcerer named Merlin, an enchanted sword called Excalibur, and the majestic lady of the lake. Depending on what version of the story you read, she is called by many names, including Vivian, Nimue, and Morgan. This spell calls upon her divine nature to assist you in overcoming obstacles and taking on more responsibility. If you are looking to be a leader in the community, bring attention to yourself, gain public recognition, or go into business on your own, then just like King Arthur, you would do well to adhere to the wisdom of the lady at the lake and take up the sword.

- Red apple
- Dish or plate
- Blade of any kind (e.g., butter knife or letter opener, to symbolize a sword)
- Blue chime candle
- 3 drops lily-of-the-valley essential oil
- Matches or lighter

1 Hold the apple between your hands, close your eyes and say, "Dearest lady of the lake, I offer you this gift to take."

2 Place the apple on the dish, stem side up. Insert the blade into the apple, entering through the top. The blade should be able to stay upright once in the apple. If the weight of the blade topples the apple, hold it with one hand upright.

3 Once the blade has pierced the apple, say, "Grant me courage, grant me favor, don't let my strength and leadership waver."

4 Close your eyes and grasp the hilt of the blade. Imagine all the obstacles you're currently facing or will face as you pursue this next step. Imagine that you're wielding a magnificent sword and cutting through all the obstacles and negative energies.

5 Cut the apple in half and place the two halves on the dish.

6 Anoint the blue candle with the essential oil, rubbing from the wick down toward the base. Push the candle into one of the apple halves to secure it in place.

7 Light the candle and as it burns, say, "Lady of the lake, you of many names, I honor you by lighting the sacred flame."

8 While the candle is burning, eat the other half of the apple and envision yourself being filled with the courage, strength, and power needed to achieve your goals.

9 When the candle has completely burned down, take the other apple half and bury it in your backyard, or toss it in a stream, lake, or body of water. Remember to thank the lady of the lake for her assistance.

BRIDGET'S TRIPLE THREAT OIL

Bridget is the Celtic goddess of poetry, healing, and crafting. She eventually transformed into the Catholic St. Brigid and became known in Haiti and New Orleans as Maman Brigitte. With this oil you can unlock the many aspects that are sacred to Bridget/St. Brigid/Maman Brigitte. If you are a writer, actor, artist, or someone looking to manifest a new creative endeavor, this oil will do the trick. Wear this oil behind your ears and on your wrists, and use it to anoint candles or any tools used for creative endeavors, such as pens or dance shoes.

- Almond oil
- Amber glass bottle
- 3 drops dragon's blood essential oil
- 3 drops amber essential oil
- 3 drops rosemary essential oil
- Pinch vervain
- Pinch chili flakes

1 Pour the almond oil into the amber bottle, being sure to leave a little room for the essential oils.

2 Add the dragon's blood, amber, and rosemary oils.

3 Sprinkle the vervain in the bottle and say, "Brigid, goddess, saint, and loa, I ask for your blessings and divine inspiration; enchant this oil so that it may heal."

4 Sprinkle the chili flakes in the bottle as you say, "You who hold the sacred flame, instill unto me creativity and fame."

5 Cap the lid and give it a good shake. Use it whenever you want to increase your creativity, or to help with healing. Store it in a dark place such as cupboard or drawer.

WITCH'S MAGIC MANIFESTATION BREW

You've heard of writer's block, but did you know that witches can get similarly blocked, too? We can get blocked creatively, emotionally, and spiritually. This enchanting tea blend clears away all blockages and invokes creative vibrations, as well as enhancing psychic and magical gifts. Drink this bewitching brew before bedtime and from a black mug to add to the brew's powers.

- Small bowl
- 1 tablespoon chamomile
- 1 tablespoon lemon balm
- 1 tablespoon lavender
- 1 tablespoon vanilla
- ½ teaspoon mugwort
- 8 ounces hot water
- Tea strainer or cheesecloth
- Cup (preferably a black mug)
- Milk
- Honey

1 In a small bowl, mix together all the dried chamomile, lemon balm, lemon balm, lavender, vanilla, and mugwort.

2 Steep 2 teaspoons of the tea, either in a strainer or with a cloth, in the water for about 5 minutes.

3 Strain the tea with the tea strainer or cheesecloth and pour the liquid into a cup. Sweeten it with milk and honey, as desired.

4 Find a cozy, quiet place to relax and sip your tea.

5 Close your eyes and visualize all blockages and obstacles disappearing, and your imagination and passions returning full force as you drink the brew.

DIANA'S LUNAR LOTION POTION

Diana is the ancient Roman goddess of the moon and forest, and protector of women. She is the divine huntress, and in later times became known as the goddess of witches. Witches have a strong connection to the moon, and this little potion strengthens that connection. Use this lotion whenever a spell calls for a specific lunar phase and it's not the right time, or when you wish to connect with the moon or Diana. Not only will it leave your skin feeling silky smooth, but you'll also feel your magic amplified.

- 4 drops jasmine essential oil
- 2 drops lotus essential oil
- 1 drop sandalwood essential oil
- 8 fluid ounces unscented body lotion (screw top)

1 Add the drops of jasmine, lotus, and sandalwood essential oil directly to the container of unscented lotion.

2 Mix the oils into the lotion by stirring it clockwise with your finger.

3 As you stir, say, "Diana, beloved of witches, I crave a boon; enchant this lotion with the power of the moon."

4 After you've mixed the oils in thoroughly, you can keep the lotion in the container it came in, or scoop it into another container or jar that can be properly sealed.

APHRODI-TEA

There's nothing quite like a good love potion, especially one with such a punny title. Aphrodisiacs are nature's magical stimulants for the senses, specifically the romantic and psychic kind. Like the name suggests, Aphrodite, the Greek goddess of love, romance and pleasure, rules over aphrodisiacs. Brew this cup of love on a Friday evening before a date to enhance your chances of finding a relationship, or pair it with another love spell for added potency.

- Small bowl
- 2 tablespoons dried rose petals
- 2 tablespoons dried lavender
- ½ teaspoon dried jasmine
- 1 teaspoon pure vanilla extract
- 8 ounces hot water
- Tea strainer or cheesecloth
- Cup
- Milk
- Honey

1 In a small bowl, mix together the rose petals, lavender, jasmine, and vanilla extract.

2 Add about one tablespoon of the tea from the above recipe to the hot water and let the mixture steep for at least 5 minutes.

3 Strain the tea and pour the liquid into a cup. Sweeten it with milk and honey, as desired.

4 Sip the tea and let your mind wander, thinking about love and who you wish to manifest.

"HELLO POPPET" BINDING SPELL

If you find yourself in a situation where another person is being hostile toward you, gossiping about you, or interfering with your life in a negative way, it might be appropriate to put them in a time-out. This binding will not hurt the person in question or cause them physical harm, but it will restrict them from hurting you and causing you any more grief or discomfort. Unless you want to make your own doll, you can find one at most craft stores. If making your own, simply cut out two pieces of cloth in a gingerbread man shape and sew them together, stuffing the doll with cotton filling.

- Small piece of paper (sticky-note size)
- Red pen
- Black pen
- Cloth, human-shaped doll
- 2-foot black cord
- Empty shoebox
- Black duct tape

1 Write the name of the person in question on the piece of paper with the red pen. If you know their birth date or astrological sign, write that down as well for extra potency and connection to the target.

2 With the black pen, draw 9 lines through the person's name while repeating, "Try like hell, you can't resist this spell," as you draw each line through the name.

3 Take the poppet in your hand and begin attaching the paper to the poppet by wrapping the cord around them both. If the person has been gossiping about you, cover

the face with the cord, also making sure to bind the arms and legs as well. As you bind the poppet, repeat the words, "I bind you (person's name) from doing me harm. Until you back off, you'll be bound to this charm."

4 Leave enough cord so that you can securely tie three knots as you finish binding the doll.

5 Once the poppet has been completely bound, place it in the shoebox and seal it with duct tape. Hide it in the back or your closet, garage, or attic.

6 Undo the spell at any time by retrieving the poppet and cutting the cord with scissors while saying, "I hope you had some time to think. Now it's time to break this link." Then sprinkle some salt over the poppet and burn the paper. You may cleanse the poppet with smoke, salt, and a sprinkle of water to use it again for a different person or purpose. Alternatively, you may burn the entire thing.

JUPITER'S MATERIAL MANIFESTATION RITUAL

Jupiter is king of the gods; he rules the heavens and watches mankind from afar. He likes his gold coins and other treasure. So, who better to petition when you want some sort of luxury? Get Jupiter on your side and the sky's the limit. Perform this ritual on a Thursday, a day dedicated to Jupiter.

- Red chime candle
- Matches or lighter
- Heatproof dish or plate (preferably ceramic)
- Picture or image of an eagle
- Pinch agrimony
- Pinch yarrow
- Pinch chamomile
- Something that symbolizes what you desire (e.g., keys for a new car or home, piece of paper with dollar amount written out, travel brochure, etc.)
- 1 (3-by-3-inch) piece of purple cloth
- 1 piece lapis lazuli stone (raw or tumbled)

1 Heat the bottom of the chime candle with a match and stand it on the dish.

2 Place the image of the eagle in front of the dish and candle.

3 Place both hands over the image and say, "Mighty Jupiter, lord of the sky, I call on you now, please hear me and reply."

4 Sprinkle agrimony, yarrow, and chamomile, one at a time, in a circular motion around the candle.

5 Hold both hands directly over the candle and say, "Like Medea and Circe, I use herbs for their power. Oh Jupiter, please enhance my spell in this hour."

6 Light the candle. As it burns, hold the item that symbolizes your desire and close your eyes. Focus on your intent. Imagine what it is that you want. See yourself playing on your new game console, watching a movie on your giant new television, or walking into your beautiful new home—whatever your desire may be.

7 Let the candle burn down completely.

8 Once the candle has fully extinguished, collect the herbs and any wax remnants and wrap them in the purple cloth, along with the image of the eagle and lapis lazuli.

9 Keep the bundle on your altar, by your window, or on your nightstand until you get your desire.

10 When you receive what you've manifested, thank Jupiter by burning the bundle safely and blowing the ashes out a window or front door. Bury the stone and any other remnants that refuse to burn.

WITCH'S DELICIOUS DEVIL'S FOOD CAKE

While it is a common misconception that witches worship the Judeo-Christian figure known as Satan, in traditional witchcraft and folklore, they do work with an entity or spirit often referred to as "the devil." However, he is a teacher of wisdom, and mostly a modern re-imagining of different ancient Pagan gods. Feel like you are stuck in a routine? Afraid to really practice magic or witchcraft? Perhaps you are thinking too hard and spending too much time trying to follow the rules. You'll learn how to obtain your desire by first giving into desire. Bake this boozy, moist cake.

- ◆ 1 (15.25-ounce) box devil's food cake mix
- ◆ Oil, eggs, and water (as called for in cake mix package directions)
- ◆ Silver fork
- ◆ 6 ounces dark rum
- ◆ Red birthday candle
- ◆ Matches or lighter

1 Make the devil's food cake according to the package directions.

2 After it has baked, place it on a wire rack to cool for 5 minutes and then turn the cake over.

3 With your silver fork, poke holes all over the cake while saying, "I make this cake to entice the devil; teach me the craft, for I am a rebel."

4 Pour the rum over the cake, then let it sit for about 30 minutes.

5 Cut yourself a piece of the cake and insert the birthday candle into the cut piece.

6 Light the candle and say, "Devil, now please grant my wish, and like this cake; make my life delish."

7 Close your eyes, take a deep breath, and imagine yourself free from rules and anything weighing you down. Think of your magic and what you wish to accomplish.

8 Blow out the candle and eat the slice of cake.

9 You may save the rest of the cake and keep it for yourself, or offer it to family and friends who may need to loosen up a bit.

APOLLO'S PROPHECY PILLOW

Apollo is the Greco-Roman god of healing, music, the sun, and prophecy. His sacred temple of Delphi was famous for housing priestesses known as the Pythia, who would reveal prophecies, predictions, omens, and words of wisdom. People from all over the world made the pilgrimage to this sacred temple to gain insight about things of importance to them. Create this pillow on a Sunday afternoon and sleep with it to enhance your prophetic gifts. If you have any divination tools, such as tarot, oracle cards, or a pendulum, you may place them next to, beneath, or on top of the pillow to strengthen the psychic vibrations of your tools.

- ◆ 2 (3-by-3-inch) squares of purple cloth
- ◆ Sewing needle
- ◆ Purple thread
- ◆ 3 pinches mugwort
- ◆ 3 pinches lavender
- ◆ 3 pinches lemon verbena
- ◆ 3 whole bay leaves
- ◆ 1 small amethyst
- ◆ 1 small citrine

1 Place the squares of cloth on top of each other and sew 3 sides of the cloth together using the sewing needle and purple thread.

2 Turn the pillow right side out, so that the seams you just sewed are on the inside, and fill it with the herbs and crystals, then sew it shut.

3 Hold the pillow between your hands and say, "Lord Apollo, spirit of light, please grant me the gift of sight."

4 Place the prophecy pillow inside your pillowcase while you sleep.

5 Be aware of any obscure dreams that you may have and write them down upon waking. Take time to work with your divination tools and trust your intuition.

DRUID'S VERVAIN SACHET

A sacred herb to the Druids, vervain has many magical properties, with uses that include fostering love and psychic development, offering protection, and boosting spells and magic. Being a witch or practicing witchcraft might make you the subject of ridicule, stigma, and gossip. Carry this sachet with you not only to draw on this herb's ancient power, but also to protect you against those who may wish to harm you.

- 2 (3-by-3-inch) squares of black cloth
- Sewing needle
- Black thread
- 3 tablespoons vervain
- 1 tablespoon salt

1 Place the squares of cloth on top of each other and sew three sides of the cloth together.

2 Stuff the sachet with the vervain and salt, and sew it shut.

3 Hold the sachet between your hands, close your eyes, and say, "Sacred herb of Druids and witches, protect me from gossip, malice, and bitches. Enhance my power, strengthen my magic, let those who hurt me find themselves in a state far more tragic."

WISH UPON A STAR SPELL

If you've seen Disney's Pinocchio *or read fairy tales as a child, then you have a general idea about what it means to wish upon a star. In tarot, The Star represents hope, and when pulled in a reading, it signifies that you should not give up on your dreams or goals. Perform this spell during a new moon or on a Monday evening when you want a wish to be granted, no matter how outlandish or impossible it sounds.*

- 1 stick jasmine incense
- Incense holder
- Matches or lighter
- White chime candle
- Candle holder
- The Star card from a tarot deck

1 When alone in a room in which you feel comfortable, light the incense stick, waving it around as it burns to distribute the smoke so it may purify the air and charge the space for the magic you are about to perform. Then place the incense stick in the holder.

2 Light the white chime candle.

3 Remove The Star card from a tarot deck, wave it through the incense smoke, and say, "Starlight, star bright, let my wish come true tonight."

4 Wave the card over the flame of the candle (being careful not to burn the card or yourself), and say, "Like a flame of pure desire, let my wish ignite with fire."

5 Focus on your wish while you let both the incense and candle burn down completely.

6 Place The Star card on your altar or by your nightstand, or tape it to your mirror for the next week so that you constantly see it and are reminded to remain hopeful.

DEVIL'S SHOESTRING CHARM

Devil's shoestring is an extremely popular root in southern conjure and Hoodoo that can be used in spells and charms for luck, gambling, stopping gossip, removing curses and hexes, and gaining employment or even getting a promotion. The root can be purchased at online retailers and some metaphysical stores and apothecaries. Create this charm on a Saturday and carry it with you when you need a little additional luck and want the scales to tip in your favor, such as when asking for a promotion, applying for a job, asking for a favor, or needing a favorable outcome from a decision.

- 3 pieces devil's shoestring
- Red cotton or flannel drawstring bag
- 3 coins (any kind)
- Pair of dice

1 Hold the pieces of devil's shoestring in your hand and say, "I shake the devil by his tail, and with his luck I shall prevail." Place it in the bag.

2 Hold the three coins and say, "Three times three and nine times nine, let what I desire be mine," and then add the coins to the bag.

3 Hold the dice in your hand and say, "In my favor would be nice, thrice about I throw the dice," and then add the dice to the bag.

4 Close the bag, sealing it with three knots.

HEKATE'S SKELETON KEY

Hekate is one of the oldest deities associated with witch-craft. A primordial Titan from ancient Greece, she is the goddess of the moon, underworld, witchcraft, and the crossroads, and is usually depicted with three heads. If anyone can assist you with manifestation, it's her. Create this charm on a dark moon (the evening before the new moon, which is a time that is sacred to Hekate). Carry this charm with you when things seem difficult. The key of Hekate can unlock any door and overcome any obstacle. This charm can help when you need people to start saying yes instead of no. It can also assist in awakening your third eye and lifting the veil so that you can communicate with spirits and connect to your guides. Don't be surprised if you have vivid dreams after making this charm, and keep an eye out for signs from nature, as Hekate may be sending you messages.

- ◆ Matches or lighter
- ◆ 1 stick frankincense
- ◆ Incense holder
- ◆ Vintage or antique key
- ◆ 1 drop olive oil
- ◆ Small black dish
- ◆ 1 pinch lavender
- ◆ 3 crushed bay leaves
- ◆ 1 pinch barley (chamomile can be used as a substitution)

1 Using matches or a lighter, light the frankincense and place it in an incense holder.

2 Anoint the key with a drop of olive oil, then hold the key in your left hand and say, "Hekate, I invoke thee, please enchant this the sacred key."

3 Place the key on the dish. Sprinkle the lavender on the key and say, "Herb of dreams, cleansing, and renewal, revive my power and give it fuel."

4 Sprinkle the crushed bay leaves over the key and say, "Sacred herb to the god of light, enchant this key on this dark night."

5 Sprinkle the barley (or chamomile) over the key and say, "Hekate, I honor thee, and continue to as I wear this key."

6 Run the key through the incense smoke and say, "By Hekate I enchant this key. May all doors unlock for me."

7 Discard the dish of herbs in your backyard. Sleep with the key under your pillow for three consecutive nights. You may tie the key on a cord and wear it as an amulet, place it on your altar, or carry it in your pocket.

CHAPTER 7

Owning Your Manifestations

There's nothing more magical than making well . . . er . . . magic! As you become more familiar with the basic concepts of witchcraft and the spells and rituals in this book, you'll eventually become more comfortable making alterations or customizations to spells to better suit your needs. Some spells will require that they be performed on fixed days or lunar phases, but as we discussed earlier, there's always wiggle room. Need to perform a spell during a full moon? No need to wait three more weeks for the spell; do it on a Monday (Moon's Day) evening, a day associated with lunar energy and magic. This isn't cheating and will not affect the spellwork. You are still working with the proper energies, just using them in different ways.

Customizing Spells & Rituals

When you're starting out in a spiritual practice like witch-craft, it is always recommended that you adhere to the rules and guidelines. However, unless you are Wiccan (a follower and initiate of the established religion Wicca) or part of another religious group, then you really don't have to worry about the structure of your craft, because ultimately, it's *your* craft. I know some folks might feel uncomfortable modifying spells and rituals they see in books for fear that they will mess something up, or that it will taint the desired outcome. But when it comes to spellwork, it is all about the energy that comes from you. Your intention is the main ingredient.

An important thing to keep in mind is that witchcraft is a regional, folk practice built on community-based beliefs. For example, a witch in Ireland would use different ingredients in a love spell than someone would in the Caribbean. Why? Because agriculture is different, the relationship people have with plants is different, and even the spirits are different. Today, we have access to the internet, as well as metaphysical shops that cater to different spiritual and cultural beliefs, making almost any herb or crystal easily available. If we look back to the 17th century, we would find that the herbs and tools that magical practitioners used for their craft were locally sourced, and their spells required maybe one or two hard-to-come-by items that they acquired through trade or at a market. The majority of the spells used today evolved from those of earlier centuries and therefore will list items that might be rare to us now but were quite common back then. The majority of herbs and items listed in this book are fairly easy to acquire, but regardless of how accessible the items may be, it is perfectly fine to make alterations as needed.

Modifying Ingredient Lists

Some spells may require rare and poisonous herbs such as atropa belladonna (deadly nightshade) or datura (angel's trumpet). While they may be harder to come by today, in the olden days, they were easily picked right out of the garden or found in a local woodland. If you come across a spell that you wish to perform but it requires certain herbs that are rare, expensive, or dangerous, substitute that ingredient for one that is more accessible, but still potent to your working. Rosemary can be used to substitute *any* plant or herb that you can't otherwise obtain. The same goes for zoological items such as animal bones, feet, claws, fur, skin, or teeth, which can be common ingredients in rituals and spells. Many of these items *can* be found online, but before purchasing, you should make certain that they're ethically sourced. If you do not wish to use such curios for personal reasons or cannot obtain them, bloodstone is a perfect substitute for any and all animal curio. The same can be said for other items such as crystals and stones. Are you performing a spell that requires lapis lazuli but don't have it? Use clear quartz instead, as quartz can easily and successfully substitute for any crystal.

The spells contained in this book require common herbs that are popular in witchcraft. If you are new to your practice or "in the broom closet," however, you may not have access to such herbs. This is when you'll find that rosemary is your best friend. The vervain in the Vervain Manifestation Magnet (see page 111), for example, can easily be swapped with rosemary. If you're lacking a diversely hued collection of candles, a white candle can represent any color. If you don't feel comfortable speaking a spell out loud, write it down or say it in your mind. If you don't have a private backyard to bury your spell remnants, recycle them or bury them in a potted plant instead. No matter what your approach is to spellwork, always use your intuition. Is there something you'd like to add to a spell to give it a personal touch or further enhance the magic? Do it.

Making modifications or substitutions to spells fosters a comfortable and familiar relationship with tools and magical processes. For example, most rituals are meant to be theatrical, as they are partly performance, but when working alone, you can rest assured that the spirits and energies you work with still understand what it is that you wish to manifest without needing you to wave your arms dramatically for effect. This is not to say that you shouldn't put all of your effort into the ritual; rather, you can put more energy and focus into making the connection to the spirit, or the intention, than in to the performance of the ritual.

Creating Your Own Spells & Rituals

After you get the hang of performing the spells and rituals in this book, you might eventually want to try your hand at crafting your own. This will strengthen your manifestation skills, foster your connection to witchcraft, and deepen your connection to the spiritual world and energies that surround you. Following is a simple breakdown and guidelines on how to get started crafting your own spells and rituals.

Start your grimoire. A grimoire (known in Wicca as a book of shadows) is a witch's personal collection of correspondences, spells, and rituals. It is where you keep a record of your practice and what you use in your practice. Start one by writing down spells and rituals you've tried and enjoyed. You can also catalogue all your correspondences and charts in the front of the grimoire for easy reference. By creating your own grimoire, you'll have a dedicated place to reference the spells and essential information you need to make magic.

Decide your goal, purpose, or intent. What is it that you wish to achieve? Just as you learned at the beginning of this book, you'll need to identify your goal, purpose, or intent for any spell or ritual you attempt, even the ones you create on your own. Meditate on what you want and be as specific as you can.

Pick your tools and ingredients. The next step in crafting your own spell is deciding what you wish to use to conjure up your desire. Look through the correspondences of herbs and crystals to figure out what ingredients have the best associations to help you. Remember the practice of sympathetic magic and that like affects like. When choosing tools, be creative to pick ones that represent your desire. Want a new car? Why not use a Hot Wheel to represent your next new ride. Want to attract a new partner? Ken and Barbie can easily be stand-ins for your dream boo.

When's the magic moment? The next step is coordinating the right time to set things in motion. Will you perform your spell at the witching hour? What day will it be on? Use the correspondences in this book or in your grimoire to find the appropriate day and time. You may also wish to look up holidays or celebrations of significance that might corellate to what you wish to manifest.

Who will you ask and what will you say? Will you be calling on deities or spirit guides? Once you decide if you'll be implementing such spirits and energies into your ritual or spell, you will want to look to incorporate offerings, tokens, or items of significance that will attract them to your work. If you want to use words of power or chants in your spell, think about the exact wording you'll use—your words can rhyme, be spoken aloud, remain in your mind, or even just be written down.

Write it down and make it happen. An essential part of making your own spell or ritual is to write it down, on paper or, more specifically, in your grimoire. You can make it as detailed or simple as you like, just be sure to include the ingredients needed, why you chose them, the steps necessary to complete the spell, and any other key details. Once you've written it down, it's time to craft it and make it happen.

Your Practice

You are now ready to take your manifestation to the next level with the skills and tools you've learned from this book. Remember that manifestation is not simply wishing for something or wanting it desperately. You need to believe that you can get it or make something happen despite all the obstacles that stand in your way. Manifestation is believing that something will happen against all odds. If you believe it is so, then it will be so. This is where faith and imagination come into play. Do you remember playing pirates? Having a tea party? Did you ever slay a dragon as a kid? It's time to reconnect to your inner child. By strengthening your imagination, you will not only be able to manifest like a professional, but also perform spellwork like the supreme witch you are. It is a combination of the witch's desire, the imagination, and the spirit essences that reside in the chosen ingredients that deliver your intentions to the universe. However, you're the magic maker.

Enhance your manifestation skills by first allowing yourself to want things. Nothing is out of your reach. Do not allow yourself to be limited. You want to be a movie star? Make it happen. Obviously, there will be additional work that needs to be done alongside magic, such as taking acting classes, going on auditions, etc., but nothing is impossible. That is the first thing you need to accept and believe to get what you want. The next step is to stay committed. One little candle spell is not going to make you the next Lady Gaga or Denzel Washington. As stated before, you need to apply mundane work to strengthen the magical. If you really want something, work toward that goal.

When you perform spellwork, you must be fully present for it. Magic requires dedication, commitment, and engagement. And before you embark on your spellwork, make sure to learn about the lore surrounding magical tools and ingredients. Why do witches prefer one herb over another? The more you know about the tools and items you are using, the more you will connect with them, and they with you. Knowledge is power. Now focus on your intent, think of what you wish to manifest at this moment, and let the manifestation and magic begin. Life's a witch and so are you!

TABLES OF CORRESPONDENCE

CANDLE COLORS	
BLACK	Wisdom, death, renewal, and resurrection
BLUE	Peace and tranquility
BROWN	Earth, strength, balance, justice, earth magic, animal and pet spells, and nature spirits
GOLD	Abundance, prosperity, attraction, and money
GRAY	Knowledge, communication, spirit communication, neutralizing negative energy, and wisdom
GREEN	Luck, prosperity, wealth, fertility, stability, abundance, and success
INDIGO	Renewal, relaxation, reflection, and new beginnings
ORANGE	Energy, exuberance, courage, the sun, positive outcomes, job successes, and wish fulfillment
PINK	Affection, compassion, beauty, fidelity, new love, happiness, romantic relationships, monogamy, and marriage
PURPLE	Royalty, the divine, power, and the supernatural
RED	Life-force, vitality, attraction, sensuality, desire, ambition, virility, strength, birth, death, achieving goals, overcoming obstacles, and love
SILVER	Clairvoyance, motherhood, marriage, psychic work, money, financial stability, and peace,
WHITE	Life, fertility, nourishment, goodness, balance, death, and structure
YELLOW	Brilliance, joy, clarity, insight, clairvoyance, unhexing, uncrossing, protection, and guidance

HERBS	
DAMIANA	Love, sex, aphrodisiac, lust, passion, romance, and attraction
JASMINE	Moon magic, love, feminine energy, spirituality, peace, money, sexuality, and health
ROSEMARY	Protection, cleansing, love, longevity, health, and magic boost
ALLSPICE	Healing, luck, business attraction, money, and prosperity
ANGELICA ROOT	Joy, happiness, empowerment, spiritual communication, protection, and healing
ANISE	Psychic development, protection from evil, and spirit communication
BASIL	Happiness, money, confidence, love, and protection
BAY LAUREL	Wishing, success, healing, psychic visions, cleansing, wisdom, and power
CATNIP	Love, sexuality, peace, and protection of children
CINNAMON	Money, protection, energy boost, spirituality boost, success, and libido
CLOVES	Money, luck, and friendship
LAVENDER	Protection, sleep, happiness, peace, astral projection, meditation, love, and purification
LEMONGRASS	Purification, road opener, home in earth, spirit work, and cleansing
MUGWORT	Psychic powers, prophetic dreams, astral projection, everyday protection, spirit work, strength, deity work, necromancy, and divination
NUTMEG	Luck, energy boosts, money, raising vibrations, and increasing psychic awareness

PEPPER (BLACK/ WHITE)	Protection, returning to sender, grounding, and hex breaking
ROSE	Love, peace, sex, romance, beauty, and self-esteem
SAGE	Calming, longevity, wisdom, relaxation, inspiration, spiritual cleansing and fumigation
THYME	Luck, dreams, money, financial stability, and peace
VALERIAN ROOT	Love, purification, marriage, returning to sender, ritual purification, and sleep
VERVAIN	Protection, aphrodisiac, inspiration, protection, hex breaking, and spiritual protection
WORMWOOD	Prophecy, psychic development, healing, creativity, love, peace, wisdom, and ancestral magic
YARROW	Love, psychic enhancement, wisdom, courage, mental health, and clarity
FIVE FINGER GRASS/ CINQUEFOIL	Protection, purification, luck, divination, sorcery, health, and healing

OILS	
AMBER	Money, sensuality, goddess energy, psychic development, ancestral work, and protection
BERGAMOT	Money, happiness, cleansing, and peace
CYPRESS	Healing, comfort, grieving, and longevity
DRAGON'S BLOOD	Magic, power, protection, healing, luck, and spiritual clearing
EUCALYPTUS	Healing, protection, and uncrossing
FRANKINCENSE	Protection, purification, spirituality, meditation, anxiety, soothing fear, calmness, and higher consciousness

HONEYSUCKLE	Prosperity, psychic awareness, protection, sweetness of life, spiritual insight, and goal fulfillment
JASMINE	Confidence, love, sex, money, peace, spirituality, insight, and lunar magic
LOTUS	Egyptian magic, wisdom, blessings, and goddess magic
MUSK	Courage, masculine energy, fertility, attraction, lust, and sex magic
MYRRH	Protection, purification, meditation, grounding, confidence, spiritual awakening, and spiritual fumigation
ORANGE BLOSSOM	Joy, money, happiness, personal development, and banishing negative thoughts
OLIVE OIL	Purification, cleansing, divine energy, spiritual awakening, spirit work, and ritual purification
PATCHOULI	Fertility, physical energy, romance, partnership, divine self, attraction, and money
PEPPERMINT	Protection, calming, wisdom, spirituality, cleansing, happiness, and positivity stimulant
ROSE	Beauty, love, sex, peace, psychic protection, and honesty
SANDALWOOD	Wish fulfillment, healing, spirituality, protection, sexual awakening, attraction, and higher consciousness
VANILLA	Love, magic, mental awareness, energy, sex, mental health, and relationships
VIOLET	Love, wish fulfillment, healing, calmness, and peace
YLANG-YLANG	Aphrodisiac, attraction, euphoria, relaxation, bliss, love, and grounding
CINNAMON	Money, luck, courage, vitality, and success

DAYS OF THE WEEK

SUNDAY	"Sun's day"; manifestation, male energy, divine power, courage, spells for happiness, success, and job opportunities
MONDAY	"Moon's day"; [for consistency] Lunar deities, dream work, spiritual growth, psychic and divination work, healing, and cleansing
TUESDAY	"Mars day"; courage, conflict resolution, virility, and gaining wisdom or overcoming obstacles
WEDNESDAY	"Mercury's day"; self-improvement, communication, divination, travel, friendships, and spirit communication
THURSDAY	Jupiter; money, legal matters, luck, and success
FRIDAY	Venus; love, friendship, art, creativity, pleasure, and fertility
SATURDAY	Saturn; banishing, hex breaking, cleansing, healing, returning to sender, and motivation

LUNAR CYCLES

NEW MOON	New beginnings, uncovering truth, spiritual awakening, cleansing, protection of home and self, and bindings
WAXING MOON	Money spells, financial stability, job attraction, energy intensity, growth, and abundance
FULL MOON	Healing, wish fulfillment, goddess magic, prosperity, spirit work, love magic, and attraction
WANING MOON	Banishing, purging, removing negativity, protection, change, and letting go

STONES	
AGATE	Health, luck, and gambling
AMBER	Love, luck, and transformation
AMETHYST	Fighting addiction, psychic awareness, insight, healing, crown chakra, and spirit work
APACHE TEARS	Protection, comfort, ancestral magic, and cleansing
BLOODSTONE	"Stone of courage"; purification, clearing negativity, and balance
CARNELIAN	Creation, creativity, life force, fear, stability, virility, and health
CITRINE	Prosperity, abundance, money, mental focus, and endurance
HEMATITE	Health, grounding, returning to sender, relaxation, peace, and spirit work
JET	Protection, earth magic, spirit cleansing, and manifestation enhancement
JASPER	Protection and mental clarity
LAPIS LAZULI	Divine energy, protection, and health
MOONSTONE	Lunar magic, balance, reflection, new beginnings, creative energies, and increased intuition/insight
OBSIDIAN	Protection, hex breaking, grounding, and spirit work
TIGERS EYE	Grounding, creativity, wisdom, insight, emotional balance, and raising vibrations

GLOSSARY

You may find that not all these words are used in the book; however, they are in this glossary to provide a greater understanding of magic.

altar: A table or secret space that is used for ritual, sacrifices, offerings, or spellwork

amulet: An ornament or charm used to protect against evil, danger, or disease

anointing: Dressing a candle with oils

capnomancy: Divination method of using smoke after the fire has been made

conjure: American folk magic that incorporates African, Native American, Jewish, Catholic, Christian, and European traditions

consecrate: To make something sacred, typically a tool that will be used for spiritual or magical purposes

deity: A god, goddess, or divine spirit

divination: The practice of seeking knowledge of the future or the unknown through the use of tools or supernatural means

esbat: Witches' celebration of the new and full moons

grimoire: A book of magical texts usually created by a practitioner, containing correspondences, seals and sigils, spells, and other information

hex: To cast a spell or bewitch; commonly used for ill will, revenge, or with malicious intent

jinx: Bad luck, caused magically by another person, or by breaking a superstition or folk belief

juju: A practice from West Africa of incorporating objects such as amulets, spells, and talismans in religious practices

libanomancy: Divination that involves observing incense smoke

magic: The ability to subdue or manipulate energies, both natural and supernatural.

novena: From the Latin word meaning "nine," a traditional style of devotional praying in Christianity and Catholicism

omen: A sign or event that is regarded as carrying prophetic significance; can be either good or bad

Pagan: A non-Abrahamic person, possibly who adheres to old spiritual beliefs, and is not Christian, Jewish, or Muslim

poppet: A doll, usually stuffed with herbs, meant to represent someone and used for magic

purification: To cleanse, both spiritually and physically

pyromancy: Divination through the use of fire

ritual: A sequence of activities that may involve gestures, words, or actions performed for spiritual enlightenment, to gain magical momentum, and to maintain tradition

Sabbat: The holy days of the witch, of which there are eight in Wicca, including Beltane and Samhain

scrying: Gazing at various forms and surfaces that offer guidance, prophecy, and answers to potential questions through symbols and images that appear

sex magic: Any type of sexual activity used for magical, ritualistic, or spiritual purposes, usually incorporating sexual arousal with the visualization of a desired result that is powered energetically and spiritually by orgasms

sigil: Inscribed or painted symbol with magical power

spells: Magic that is conducted with the use of tools, spoken words, or rituals, including the act of crafting a charm, talisman, incense, or oil for magical purposes

talisman: An object, inscribed or handmade, that harnesses magical powers and energy

veve: Specific spiritual symbols associated with the different loas or spirits of Voodoo

vigil: A time of devotional watching or observance, typically referring to a spell or ritual that may last several hours or more than one day

Wicca: A recognized Neo-Pagan religion begun in the 1960s by British witch Gerald Gardner

witch's ladder: Cord or string knotted for magical purposes, often tied with feathers, beads, or shells, and kept as a charm or talisman

RESOURCES

SUPPLIES

Pan's Apothika (formerly Panpipes)
This is the first metaphysical shop I ever went to as a child. It carries hundreds of herbs and oils, and can custom-prepare tools of intention. Vicky, the shop owner and a dear friend, specializes in individually anointed, glass-enclosed candles, typically the seven-day candle, which is an excellent tool for manifesting one's intentions.
> PanPipes.com
> (323) 891-5936

III Crows Crossroads
Offering charmed essentials for everyone, this company was started by two of my fellow coven members and blends together the magic of traditional witchcraft, Voodoo, Santeria, and American folk conjure. Here, you'll find soaps, candles, oils, spell kits, and many more enchanting items to get you started on your spiritual journey.
> @3crowscrossroads
> Etsy.com/shop/IIICrowsCrossroads

The Olde World Emporium
My very own brick-and-mortar shop in Santa Clarita, carrying a vast collection of stones, crystals, books, and tarot decks, plus a fully stocked apothecary for all your magical needs.
> @theoldeworldemporium
> OldeWorldEmporium.com

PODCASTS

Life's A Witch
A podcast that I co-host with my friend, Ivy, during which we discuss daily life as a witch, obstacles we face, spells, and cultural events, and have lots of laughs. Available on all major streaming platforms.

The Witch and the Medium
I cohost this podcast with famed medium Adela Lavine. Together, we talk about our different practices, gifts, and beliefs, and share our experiences with the supernatural and knowledge on different topics each week.
@thewitchandthemedium
TheWitchAndTheMedium.com

Bigfoot Collectors Club
A paranormal podcast hosted by Michael McMillian and Bryce Johnson that explores ghost sightings, folklore, historical anomalies, the occult, and high strangeness.
@bigfootcollectorsclub

BOOKS

The Voodoo Hoodoo Spellbook by Denise Alvarado
This book is a wonderful resource filled with history, authentic spells, recipes, and more—all focusing on the Voodoo practiced in New Orleans.

The Master Book of Herbalism by Paul Beyerl
Probably the best book on herbs available for a magical practitioner, it offers in-depth information about herb lore, oils, incense, elixirs, and uses for magic.

Encyclopedia of Witchcraft **by Judika Illes**
This is a must-have for all practitioners, as well as those interested in learning more about witchcraft. Whether you're looking for information on a deity, tool, specific practice, or history, this book has it.

The Element Encyclopedia of Secret Signs and Symbols **by Adele Nozedar**
A great resource for looking up symbols you may see in wax, dreams, clouds, etc.

Mastering Witchcraft **by Paul Huson**
One of the very first books on witchcraft I read that was not Wiccan. This book aligns more with traditional witchcraft and focuses more on witchcraft as a practice. It's a truly wonderful resource.

REFERENCES

Barrett, Francis. *The Magus: A Complete System of Occult Philosophy.* Newburyport, MA: Red Wheel Weiser, 2000.

Blavatsky, H. P., and Michael Gomes. *The Secret Doctrine: The Classic Work, Abridged and Annotated.* New York: Jeremy P. Tarcher/Penguin, 2009.

Dell, Christopher. *The Occult, Witchcraft and Magic: An Illustrated History.* London: Thames & Hudson, 2016.

Hennessey, Kathryn, ed. *A History of Magic, Witchcraft, and the Occult.* New York: Dorling Kindersley Publishing, Incorporated, 2020.

Hurst, Katherine. "Law of Attraction History: The Origins of The Law of Attraction Uncovered." TheLawOfAttraction.com. Accessed May 13, 2021. thelawofattraction.com/history-law-attraction-uncovered.

INDEX

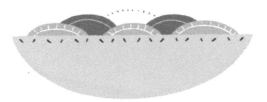

SPELLS & RITUALS
INDEX

Acknowledgments

I'd like to thank Ashley Popp, Sean Newcott, and Rockridge Press for the opportunity to write a second book!

To my parents, Steven and Ingrid, my brother Al, and my grandmother, Mom-Cat (a.k.a. Lillian), who supported my interest in witchcraft.

To Lana, Leah, and Brenna, who took me in as their kin, plus let me throw cards and cast spells for them.

To Joel Castillo, my dear friend who started me on my path to becoming a professional witch.

To Heather, Morgan, and Steve, who continuously offer me their kindness and support.

To Ivy Hedge, who helped me write this book when I broke my finger and didn't mind my whining.

To Cyndi, Jess, Vicky of Panpipes, Nyt Myst, Bloody Mary, Adela Lavine, and my many other magical mentors and friends, and of course my ancestors and spirits—thank you.

About the Author

 **Mystic Dylan** is also the author of *Candle Magic for Beginners: Spells for Prosperity, Love, Abundance, and More*. His love of knowledge allowed him to study, explore, and dedicate himself to the art of traditional witchcraft.

He has worked professionally as a witch and spiritual consultant for over 10 years. He currently lives in Los Angeles, California, where he teaches classes and owns his own shop, The Olde World Emporium.